Morning Resolve

Morning Resolve

To Live a Simple, Sincere, and Serene Life

*Thank you for joining me on the
quest for simple, sincere, & serene life!*

Patrick Allen

Patrick Allen

foreword by
Canon Scott Gunn

CASCADE *Books* · Eugene, Oregon

MORNING RESOLVE
To Live a Simple, Sincere, and Serene Life

Cascade Books
An Imprint of Wipf and Stock Publishers
199 W. 8th Ave., Suite 3
Eugene, OR 97401

www.wipfandstock.com

ISBN 13: 978-1-4982-2354-6

Cataloguing-in-Publication Data

Allen, Patrick.

    Morning resolve: To live a simple, sincere, and serene life / Patrick Allen; foreword by Canon Scott Gunn.

    xviii + 160 p. ; 23 cm.

    ISBN 13: 978-1-4982-2354-6

    1. Spiritual life—Christianity. 2. Prayer—Christian. 3. Forward Movement. I. Title.

BV4501.2 A341 2015

Manufactured in the USA.   11/16/2015

As the provost of several very fine Christian universities, I have had the privilege of serving with a number of extraordinary theologians and biblical scholars. They have certainly shaped my understanding of Scripture and theology in profound ways. I owe each one a huge debt of gratitude. However, their influence pales in comparison to that of my wife, Lori. She has shown me more about the love of Jesus and compassion for my neighbors than I can possible put into words. I dedicate *Morning Resolve* to her in acknowledgement of her love, support, and encouragement over the past fifteen years. This book simply could not have been written without her.

For me, it all comes down to this:
Life is messy, but God is faithful.

Contents

PART III—Exercising Graceful Activities

PART IV—Practicing Faithful Habits

Foreword

A FEW YEARS AGO, I began a new ministry serving as the leader of Forward Movement, publishers of *Forward DAY by DAY*. As part of my ministry, I travel widely throughout the Episcopal Church, quite often visiting churches to speak about discipleship or sometimes the work of Forward Movement.

On these trips, it is quite common for people to tell me their "*Forward DAY by DAY* story." I hear stories about how a simple daily devotional—updated a bit, but recognizable to its 1935 origins—has been an instrument to change lives. People tell me how a particular reading gave them hope when they needed it, or perhaps it gave them courage to do something extraordinary.

More than once, a person has walked up to me and recited, verbatim, "A Morning Resolve." Sometimes people will refer to a phrase from the prayer (maybe "a childlike faith in God") in conversation. I think people tell me these things because they want me to know how important *Forward DAY by DAY* and its prayers are to them.

This short prayer, just 133 words, is a solid foundation on which to build the activities, hopes, and plans for one's day. It's not surprising that this short, powerful prayer would work its way into the spiritual lives of so many people, because it brings together so many crucial themes for living well.

What would our world be like if more of us had habits of holy silence or carefulness in conversation? How much would our lives improve if we could successfully repel discontent and discouragement? As the prayer itself calls to our minds, we can do none of these things on our own. We rely on God's grace for transformation.

This prayer has a global fan base, and with good reason. I have heard the stories from dozens or even hundreds of people around the world. Perhaps you too have been strengthened by "A Morning Resolve," or perhaps you are looking for new direction in your life.

The book you are about to read is a magnificent and rich resource to open for us new paths for God's grace in our lives. Built on the structure of a powerful prayer, we readers are taken on a great journey through Patrick Allen's own spiritual journey. In all this we see new ways that we might grow in our own walk with Jesus Christ. Here are examples, successes, failures, scriptural teachings, and questions for deep pondering.

Dr. Allen has given us a great gift. I am grateful to know that I can recommend this book to thousands of people who already know "A Morning Resolve," and I hope many thousands more will find their way to patterns of daily prayer and study in these pages.

I commend this book to you. It is well worth careful reading in its own right, and it draws us deep into a very rich prayer. Even more than this, we readers may see and learn new ways for God to work in and through our lives.

The Reverend Canon Scott Gunn

Executive Director,
Forward Movement

Preface

I GREW UP IN a religious tradition that did not talk much about spiritual disciplines or discipleship. We were told that it is one thing to become a Christian, but something altogether different to become a holy person. That was clear. What was not so clear, however, was how we were to go about becoming a mature Christian. The focus was on all the things we were *not* to do—dance, smoke, drink, wear makeup, go to movies, play games with dice or face cards, and many more. Certainly, the list of what not to do was daunting. What was missing, of course, was any discussion about what spiritual disciplines (other than prayer and church attendance) we could practice with the goal of formation. We had no language for that. It wasn't until I accepted a faculty post at Friends University that I took spiritual disciplines seriously. Richard Foster was on faculty there, and his recently released book, *Celebration of Discipline*, was enormously helpful to me. I learned much from Richard, too, and I have always been thankful for the time he spent with this young colleague. I began to see how spiritual formation could be intentional and purposeful, and over the years I have tried to be both.

For the past ten years or so, my wife, Lori, and I have been reading some of the daily prayers found in *Forward DAY by DAY*, a daily devotional published by Forward Movement, as part of our daily spiritual discipline. We always start with "A Morning Resolve." This prayer has helped us navigate some very dark times; we have learned to quote it by heart.

And more recently, I taught a course on spiritual disciplines to doctoral students. I was taken by how much they enjoyed learning about and practicing these disciplines, and I was surprised by how little they knew about them. They reminded me so much of me at that age! As I thought about it, it came to me that "A Morning Resolve" could be used as a cen-terpiece for small groups or individuals who are seriously interested in crafting a simple, sincere, and serene life by putting into practice many of the activities mentioned in the prayer. It is my hope that this book will be a good way to productively embrace these healthy spiritual practices. You will have to judge the extent to which my efforts have been successful.

My prayer is that you will be challenged, shaped, and formed by the practices found herein, and that you will recognize God's fingerprints all over your life. I suggest that you read the prayer in its entirely every day, and focus on one chapter of the book each week. And please find someone or a small group and do this together. Spiritual formation, as it turns out, can be a team sport, and fun, too!

Just one final note—I have come to be known as a storyteller, and am often asked these questions: "Was that story true? Did that really happen?" You will find some of my stories throughout this book, and these same questions may come to mind. Most of the stories happened just the way I describe them. A few have been modified or merged together to shield the identity of the participants. And in a case or two, I tell the story just the way I remember it, but I must confess that my family and friends may remem-ber it differently. This is no attempt at fraud; rather, it is simply the result of the passing of time and perhaps a faulty memory. On whose part, I honestly do not know. In any case, the stories are true (that is, there is much truth for the taking) whether they happened just the way I remember them or not.

Acknowledgments

I WOULD BE REMISS if I didn't acknowledge the affirmation and support I have received over the years from friends, colleagues, and students (past and present) for my stories. As any storyteller will tell you, a good story is not possible without a receptive audience. Thank you to all who took the time to listen, and an even bigger thank you to those who had to listen to some of them more than once.

Introduction

I will try this day to live a simple, sincere, and serene life, repelling promptly every thought of discontent, anxiety, discouragement, impurity, and self-seeking; cultivating cheerfulness, magnanimity, charity, and the habit of holy silence; exercising economy in expenditure, generosity in giving, carefulness in conversation, diligence in appointed service, fidelity to every trust, and a childlike faith in God.

In particular I will try to be faithful in those habits of prayer, work, study, physical exercise, eating, and sleep which I believe the Holy Spirit has shown me to be right.

And as I cannot in my own strength do this, nor even with a hope of success attempt it, I look to thee, O Lord God my Father, in Jesus my Savior, and ask for the gift of the Holy Spirit.

WE ARE ALL, EACH of us, on a spiritual journey, and along the journey we pray. In fact, we pray one of two prayers. Sometimes we pray for guidance in tending our spiritual gardens so they will flourish and bear good fruit; and at other times, we simply pray for divine help to get through the day as we travel the road of disappointment, discouragement, and disillusionment. We either pray to flourish in our place or we pray with no particular place to flourish. Sometimes we pray both prayers in the course of the same day. I know I have. "A Morning Resolve," the prayer leading off this Introduction and printed on the inside front cover of *Forward DAY by DAY*, a daily devotional with lectionary readings provided by the publishing arm of the Episcopal Church, is a "help me tend my spiritual garden" prayer. It asks for God's help in living a simple, sincere, and serene life—by repelling negative thoughts and attitudes, cultivating positive attitudes, exercising graceful activities, practicing faithful daily habits, and depending on God for the strength and will to do so. I believe that God wants all of us to establish and sustain a vibrant spiritual garden, to plant, cultivate, and bear good fruit. I invite you to pray this prayer with me each morning and reflect on a portion of the prayer each week, examining and incorporating spiritual disciplines and practices that invite God's life and light to become tangible where you live, work, and serve. Let's work together to tend our spiritual gardens, seeing them grow and flourish in graceful and unexpected ways.

I will try this day to live a simple, sincere, and serene life . . .

There are several operative phrases in this remarkably short yet complex declaration. The first one is *I will try this day.* I will try. That's why resolve—to agree, to undertake, to commit, to doggedly determine—is in the title of the prayer. It is a daily commitment you make to God. You won't always be a perfect promise keeper but you will try each day, this day. That's the key. And if you stumble, then get up as best you can and keep moving. You aren't promising to be perfect, but you are promising to be faithful. As an old proverb puts it, "Pray to God but keep rowing towards shore." You promise to stay in the boat and row! And I find it easier to row with someone else in the boat, pulling on the other oar. There is no need to do this alone. I encourage you to find a close friend or small discipleship group and work through this prayer together. You can make your spiritual growth a team sport rather than a marathon. For some of us, however, tending a spiritual garden is a personal and private activity. For others, it is much easier to work in a community garden. Both approaches have their benefits; so find the approach that is most helpful to you. This book is written to be beneficial in either context.

The second operative phrase is *to live a simple, sincere, and serene life.* Wow! That's what we're all after, the spiritual fruit of a life faithfully and gracefully lived. What the "Morning Resolve" makes clear, however, is that growth doesn't just happen with a wish and a prayer; there is honest work to be done—disciplines to employ and practices to exercise. A garden won't bear good fruit without constant care—tilling, planting, feeding, weeding, and trimming—all before the harvest. In the first two parts of this journey together, we will focus on cultivating a sense of serenity in our lives. Our attention in Part I will be on consciously repelling forms of negativity such as discontent, anxiety, discouragement, impurity, and self-seeking that act like noxious weeds to choke out growth. These weeds have to be pulled. Then, in Part II, we will turn our attention to planting and tending some helpful attitudes and activities that are highlighted in the prayer—cheerfulness, magnanimity, charity, and the habit of holy silence.

We will consider elements of a sincere life in Part III, examining and exercising a set of authentic activities that bring substance and character to our spiritual walk: economy in expenditure, diligence in appointed service, fidelity to every trust, and a childlike faith in God. These disciplines will engender genuine peace and harmony, a rich and fruitful soil for spiritual growth.

Finally, we will examine some daily practices that simplify our lives, the fundamentals of personal care and spiritual growth: prayer, work, study, physical exercise, eating, and sleep. These basics are like tilling and tending the soil. Plants will simply not grow with vigor in hard or depleted soil. It is easy to overlook the importance of these daily practices. They aren't as glamorous as going on a mission trip, leading a spiritual retreat, or playing guitar on the worship team, but they are so very important if you want to see your spiritual garden flourish. We'll address these practices in Part IV. We will end with the admission that it is through God's grace that any of this is possible, and that spiritual growth is both a gift and a disciplined effort in which God partners with us.

So, let's begin our consideration of the spiritual disciplines and practices that shape and form a more simple, sincere, and serene life. An unexpected adventure awaits all of us. Onward and upward!

Repelling Negativity

Discontent, Anxiety, Discouragement, Impurity, and Self-Seeking

The Other Road—A Story

When Pharaoh let the people go, God did not lead them on the road through the Philistine country, though that was shorter.

—EXODUS 13:17

THIS IS A STORY about traveling on the other road. You think you're doing all the right things—exactly what God wants you to do, what you feel called to do, but your plans don't work out. You find yourself traveling another road. Have you been there? The truth of the matter is that at some point in our lives, we've all been there—or will be. Here's my story.

When I graduated from college, all I really wanted to do was to be involved in an organized basketball program in some way—any way. Basketball was my favorite sport, a sport in which I lettered in both high school and college. Honestly, I had my heart set on trying to catch on with an NBA team but a kind scout took me aside and told me that wouldn't happen.

"Son," he said as he looked me straight in the eyes, "you have great desire, a strong work ethic, an accurate shot, a coachable attitude, and a true love for the game. That's all good, but you lack one basic thing—the physical ability to play at the next level." Needless to say, that one missing thing proved to be essential and spelled the end of my NBA dreams.

I went to work for a college as a part-time housing director on the student life staff and worked at a local bank to make ends meet. Just before the start of basketball season, the head coach approached me and asked if I would be interested in serving as his assistant, even though the hours were long and the pay was minimal (in fact, nonexistent). I honestly didn't care. To be working with college students and spending time on the courts was truly an answer to prayer. Life was good. I was going to be a coach and I felt very close to God!

Truthfully, the team wasn't all that good, but it didn't matter. I was doing exactly what I wanted to do, exactly what I felt called to do, living life in the sweet spot. At the end of our third year together, the head coach called me into his office and told me that he had accepted a coaching position in another state. He said that I could join him but he didn't think that I would accept. He was right. I was in the middle of a graduate program and working full time at the college. A big move just wasn't possible. He anticipated my answer and told me that he had already recommended me for the head coaching position, and the college president and athletic director were very interested. He advised me to make an appointment with the president as soon as possible. I was sitting in the president's office in less than sixty minutes. It was all so exciting.

The president told me that he had been watching me for the past three years and he felt I was ready for the assignment. However, since I worked on the student life staff and would miss some office time for basketball recruiting and road trips, I needed the support and approval of my boss, the dean of students, before we could talk seriously about the job. I made my way as quickly as possible to my boss's office. When I told him of my good fortune, he just started to frown and shake his head. "It just won't work," he grumbled. "We need you here in the office. If you're gone I'll have to double up on my work and I simply can't do that. So you will need to decide—either be the head basketball coach (paying $2,500 per year) or be the associate dean of students (providing an apartment, food, and quite a bit more than $2,500 per year)." The choice was obvious, but painful nonetheless. I went back to the president, thanked him for his confidence in me, and declined the offer. My hope was that the next head coach would want me to stay on as his assistant.

Several weeks later, the college held a news conference to introduce the new head basketball coach. I slipped into the back of the room to watch the proceedings. The president stepped up to the mic and announced that they had found the perfect candidate for the job. He turned to his left and pointed to the new head coach, my boss, the dean of students. I was absolutely stunned! I couldn't believe it, and I felt betrayed and very much alone. I realized that while he was off on recruiting and road trips, I would be the one in the office answering the phones and picking up the slack. It just wasn't fair. I had a full-time job myself. And it took me awhile but it eventually hit me that since I would be doing some of the dean's job so he could coach, I would not be able to continue to work as the assistant coach either. Someone had to stay in the office, so I was out of coaching altogether. I was no longer stunned; now I was angry. So much for God's plan—thank you very much.

* * *

We will pick up this story again at the end of Part I, after chapter 5. Suffice it here to say that I had some negativity to negotiate, some bad weeds to pull—disappointment, discouragement, discontent, and perhaps an impure thought or two. Most of us do from time to time. Dealing with negativity will be the focus of the first five chapters of this book.

Discontent

I hear an almost inaudible but pervasive discontent with the price we pay for our current materialism. And I hear a fluttering of hope that there might be more to life than bread and circuses.

—BILL MOYERS

Introduction

THE FIRST PART OF this book deals with negativity and our resolve each morning to repel it, the conscious choice we make to move on and keep going. However, we are not talking here about deep emotional traumas and psychological challenges that require professional help. They are very real, of course, but beyond the scope of this book. While this reading may be helpful it is no substitute for professional assistance. It is important to use good judgment about the care you need.

In this chapter we will take a closer look at discontentment. It can be a serious stumbling block to spiritual growth and it begs a lot of questions. Is there something wrong with me when things don't work out? Is God mad at me? Did I do something wrong? Did God plan this for some reason? Of course, these are very honest questions with no simple answers. For now, let's take a closer look at various states and stages of discontent, make the distinction between shame and guilt, consult Scripture for insight, and look at several practical strategies for dealing with periods of discontent in our lives. Hopefully, along the way, we'll answer some of your questions, too.

The first thing to say is that feeling discontent with present circumstances is not necessarily a bad thing. For example, for students in high school or college to come down with senioritis, an ebbing of motivation and desire to go to class, read books, take tests, and write papers in the late spring of their senior year, is quite typical. Near the end of any long process, motivation can wane. It signals a certain readiness to move on to the next thing. This is normal. The problem comes when you have senioritis in the middle of your sophomore year or you don't have the discipline to recognize the malady for what it is and go to class and write your final papers anyway.

And there are times when you feel discontent, edgy about your work, bored, and ready for a new challenge or change of scenery. This isn't necessarily bad either. In fact, it may signal a time of transition ahead. In such times, I have received and accepted job offers and voluntary assignments that I would not have even considered at other times. I see it as a gift from God. Because I had a certain discontent with my present circumstances, I was ready for and open to consider other opportunities. Discontent can serve as a staging area for growth and change. This is what I call healthy discontent—a restless feeling that prepares you for what is ahead. It is to be recognized, appreciated, and embraced. It helps you lean in when new possibilities and opportunities come your way.

However, discontent can become unhealthy, too, bringing feelings of disappointment about how things are going or dissatisfaction with circumstances that lead to resentment, envy, and bitterness. These nasty weeds will overrun your spiritual garden in a New York minute. When they crop up, they must be pulled immediately. That's why we pray each morning: "repelling *promptly* every thought of discontent." It is a conscious decision you make, and you get better at repelling with practice—but you have to pay attention.

Disappointment and dissatisfaction are close cousins, related but not identical, much like guilt and shame. Guilt is the sense that you have done something wrong and shame is the sense that something is wrong with you. In the same way, disappointment comes when someone or something (or you) doesn't live up to your expectations. Of course, it is important to be sure that your expectations are reasonable, particularly so because we so often hold others to a much higher standard than we do ourselves, and it is important to ask if your expectations are even necessary at all. Unreasonable and unnecessary expectations set you up for disappointment every time. You say to yourself, "If she does that, then I will really be disappointed," or "if that doesn't happen, that's it. I'll really be angry at God." In essence, you have programed yourself to react in a certain way before anything happens. You just act out the part, even when the script is a negative and hurtful one. And to be honest, you not only set yourself up for disappointments; in some sad way, you actually enjoy it, too. That is, you receive some sort of payoff when you act out the drama. It is a bad weed, indeed.

Dissatisfaction comes when you feel that things aren't fair or meaningful, that you've drawn the short straw. It is so easy to get caught up in chasing the corner office, a bigger house, a better address, a nicer car or more of them, finer clothes, a cooler phone, or a better look. You try to authenticate your worth in a materialistic culture where the highest values are appearance, achievement, and affluence by looking better, doing more, and having more. That's how success is measured and others are valued, and if you're not careful that's how you will measure and value yourself, too. But since someone always has more, does more, and looks better, the end result is dissatisfaction. You can never win this arms race, and even in the race there is a deep abiding empty feeling that surely there must be more to life than bread and circuses. Honestly, the good news is that there is. As you pray and practice the "Morning Resolve," you will begin to focus on the *more* in life. Your first assignment is to recognize and quickly repel every thought of discontent.

You can go through life feeling that things are just not fair, what I call "if-only" syndrome. If only I was taller, or more talented, or better looking. If only my parents were richer or I was born in a different place. If only I had invested in that company or applied for that job. If only my boss would recognize and affirm my contributions to this company. If only God would bless me and make me special. If only I were more popular or lucky. If only. If only. If only. You can see how if-only syndrome is circular and destructive. If-only thinking feeds on itself and incubates regret. In fact, it *is* regret in action, and it legitimates envy. And when regret and envy are at work, bitterness will soon follow. This is not rich soil for spiritual growth.

Scripture

What can we learn about dealing with discontent from Scripture? Let's look at Philippians 4:11–12: "I have learned to be content whatever the circumstances. I know what it is to be in need, and I know what it is to have plenty. I have learned the secret of being content in any and every situation, whether well fed or hungry, whether living in plenty or in want. I can do all this through him who gives me strength." I think it is important to note that the writer of this passage, Paul, is in prison at the time. He is not writing from a summer vacation home on the coast. He is in chains, yet he makes three things perfectly clear. First, he has learned to be content. Contentment is a learned state, and you can learn it, too. That's good news! The learning starts when you recognize disappointment and dissatisfaction and repel those thoughts promptly when they first crop up. If you don't, they take root quickly.

Second, Paul makes it clear that he learned the secret of being content in any and every situation, not just when things were going his way. In response to a devotional about how God had blessed someone with a new home, I heard the retreat leader say, "Isn't God good when he comes through for you!" Well, yes, God is good—but God is good all the time, not just when God "comes through for you." Far too often, we confuse being fortunate with being holy. One does not require or bring the other. Being rich does not make you holy and being holy does not guarantee that you will be rich and famous or in good health or the most popular person at work. And you are no less holy or less important because you wear used clothing or have a tight budget or no job at all. Things are different in God's economy, and Paul affirms that contentment is not tied to circumstances. That's an important lesson to learn. In God's economy, the centerpiece is not appearance, achievement, and affluence—it's grace.

Furthermore, contentment is tied to the character of God. "I can do all things *through him* who gives me strength." Ultimately, it is important to remember that God is the source of your strength. You don't have to do this on your own. And where is God when things are messy? Has he forsaken you? Did you do something wrong? Is he out to get you? No, he's right there in the mess with you, working for good. It doesn't mean that the mess is good, but you can count on the reality that God is good and always present.

Some Practical Advice

I want to end this chapter with some practical advice for pulling weeds of discontent. First, experiencing tough times can be very lonely. Whatever path you're walking, it is simply better to walk it with someone else. We tend to hide, perhaps out of shame or guilt, but it is precisely at those times when we most need to be with other people—a trusted friend or a spiritual director or even a small group. Don't go it alone.

Take care of yourself. Be sure to eat and sleep properly. In AA, you are cautioned about the poor decisions you make when you are hungry, angry, lonely, or tired (HALT). When you are in HALT Mode, you will find that discontent is much harder to recognize and repel. In fact, you might find it a welcome friend if you don't have others to honestly share with and be accountable. HALT Mode is dangerous. Avoid it if you possibly can.

During tough times it is difficult to remember: This too shall pass. It may be a season but it is not your entire life. During the storm, it is okay to take cover but look ahead to better times. Things can improve. While some may scoff at your optimism, it costs you nothing and means so much. You have my permission to look forward to better days. When thoughts of discontent arise, repel them quickly. No thank you, not today. It is far easier to weed the garden when the weeds first come up.

Finally, when things aren't going well and you can't see very far down the road, it can still be a time of preparation for things to come. I believe that God honors honest preparation even when the way ahead is unclear and you feel you're traveling the wrong road. In difficult times, you can take a class, learn to garden, or build cabinets. You can get involved in a neighborhood organization or coach little league. Even when the way ahead is unclear, I simply say, lean into preparation. Find something to do or learn, or look for an organization that needs help. As the Quakers say, "Way will open in front of you and Way will close behind you." In other words, do something constructive every day. When you least expect it, life has a way of leveling out. Be hopeful—and be ready.

Conclusion

Discontentment can lead to disappointment and dissatisfaction, and they, in turn, give rise to regret, envy, and bitterness. These are, indeed, noxious weeds, and they must be pulled quickly or they will spread and choke your spiritual growth. That is why you resolve each morning to try to repel promptly every thought of discontent. Hopefully, you found good news in the fact that contentment can be learned and practiced in any circumstance, and you deal with whatever comes in God's strength—not your own. And there is some practical wisdom for walking through tough times: don't go it alone, take care of your basic needs (HALT), choose to look to better times, and prepare even with no particular end in sight. Life has a way of finding you. Be ready.

In the coming chapters, we will deal in turn with anxiety, discouragement, impurity, and self-seeking. Then, we will turn our attention to cultivating healthy spiritual practices such as cheerfulness, magnanimity, charity, and the habit of holy silence. Before we leave this chapter, however, I want to offer you a few questions for consideration. I recommend that you find someone or a small group and discuss these questions together. Truly, spiritual growth can be a communal act. When God looked at Adam (as recorded in Genesis), it was clear that it wasn't good for Adam to make his way alone. I don't think it's good for us either.

Questions for Discussion and Reflection

1. Can you point to times of healthy discontent in your life? How did God work to bring about renewal?

2. Do you find yourself disappointed by other people? How do you respond? Do you ever set yourself up for a scripted negative response? How can you avoid that particular circle dance?

3. Which aspect of our materialistic culture (appearance, affluence, achievement) hooks you the easiest? What is the result? What are the key aspects of God's economy? How does that make a difference in the way you live?

4. Do you think you can learn to be content in any circumstance? What would be the key to doing so?

5. What is your biggest takeaway from this chapter? What will you resolve to do differently starting right now? Be specific.

I will try this day to live a simple, sincere, and serene life, repelling promptly every thought of discontent . . .

— 2 —

Anxiety

Our anxiety does not empty tomorrow of its sorrows, but only empties today of its strengths.

—*CHARLES H. SPURGEON*

Introduction

ANXIETY IS NOT NORMAL, and it is not helpful either. Honestly, it's a major inhibitor to spiritual growth, just a bad habit. Anxiety is like running on a treadmill. You work up a good sweat and get your heart rate up, but you don't go anywhere. When you finish, you look up and see that you're right where you started. If you need a workout, a treadmill is fine, but if you want to go somewhere it just won't cut it. And we do want to go somewhere—we want to craft a simple, sincere, and serene spiritual life. To do so, we'll have to deal with anxiety, and we will in this chapter.

But first, an acknowledgement is in order. I realize that anxiety can be a very serious mental struggle. My heart goes out to those who deal with generalized anxiety, panic, social anxiety, obsessive compulsive disorder, post-traumatic stress, separation, or other forms of anxiety disorders. These are serious and most often require professional assistance. Getting better is a long and often painful process. I know that anxiety disorders can inhibit spiritual growth, and I also know of many who have grown spiritually in spite of or while dealing with these disorders. God is at work in all of this. In this chapter, however, I want to consider the kind of anxiety that we, all of us, deal with from time to time, and focus on the two most common weeds that show up in our spiritual gardens—fear and worry.

Fear

The first thing to say about fear, of course, is that it isn't bad all of the time. In fact, in many situations, fear is the normal and appropriate reaction. It is the alarm bell that goes off when you find yourself in a situation where harm is imminent, and a healthy fear keeps you from going into dark alleys in the first place—whether the alleys are physical or spiritual. Fear can be a good thing when it protects you, but when fear becomes excessive or inappropriate, it can rob you of strength, joy, and peace—things that feed your spiritual garden. Fear becomes, in effect, a bad weed.

Unhealthy fear comes in many shapes and sizes, but I want to focus on three of the most common weeds: fear of the unknown, fear of failure, and fear of God. We often fear those things outside our own control or understanding. When ancient map makers drew the world, there were many parts of the globe that were yet unknown. So, in the middle of the ocean, they drew a picture of a sea monster and wrote, "Here Be Dragons!" It was a warning to travelers that the unknown can be dangerous, so steer clear and stay close to shore. Fortunately, there were explorers who saw the dragons on the map as an invitation to adventure rather than something to avoid. And in doing so, they discovered new worlds. There's a lesson there for all of us. We have dragons in our lives, too.

So, what are the dragons that we avoid today? One is other people, avoiding the stranger. As a farmer in the hills of Tennessee put it to me, "Better to stick with your own people, the people you know. Who knows what troubles outsiders will bring?" Yes, who knows? And who knows the many opportunities to learn, grow, share, and serve we sacrifice because we stay in our own neighborhoods, with our own families, in our own churches? When we see the stranger as an outsider, he or she becomes a dragon we avoid, marginalize, and make invisible. We distort the world, and in doing so we stunt our own spiritual growth. If we see the world through the eyes of fear, we see outsiders as somehow less than us, and we can justify just about anything—isolation, hunger, poverty, segregation, suffering, even death. It becomes their problem, not ours. Fear of the other helps to justify an insulated, disconnected life.

Fear also keeps us from embracing other cultures and experiences, and from learning from them, too. It is an extension of the fear of the stranger, but applied to entire groups of persons. Fear of the stranger keeps us from extending hospitality to others and fear of other cultures keeps us from experiencing their hospitality, too, which can be a spiritual gift. We avoid going to non-English-speaking countries, or even parts of our own town. Like the Tennessee farmer, we keep to ourselves. But in doing so, we lose opportunities to connect to others, to enjoy their foods and traditions, to worship together, and to learn that there are other ways of doing things and seeing things—even in our relationship with God. It is a rich experience that pulls us out of our own self-selected and self-centered theology, and challenges our false sense of superiority. It is indeed fertile soil for spiritual growth, but far too often our fears keep us sitting on our own back porch and out of the community garden.

There is one other fear of the unknown that is worth mentioning—the fear of learning. Why is there such fear of learning something new? Part of it is the fear of failure that we will address next, but I think there's more to it than that. There is a fear that we might find out that what we think—or believe—is not 100 percent accurate or complete. As one student told me while complaining about a freshman-level Bible course, "I only want to be taught what I already believe." Really! It is funny and a bit sad, but honestly, we do this, too. We only want to read books, hear sermons, sing songs, and talk with folk who agree with what we already believe. The fear of learning stems from the possibility that others may think differently, and we might just be exposed to it or influenced by it—and we might have to change. It's a fear that keeps us thinking and believing in a very tight circle. If I don't think, I won't have to change; and if I don't want to change, I won't have to think. This is particularly true when it comes to our understanding of God—our theology. Many would rather try to change reality to adjust to their theology than the other way around. When this happens, fear impedes spiritual growth.

A second major fear is our fear of failure. We live in a culture of superheroes, a cult of perfection. No one remembers or celebrates who finished second in anything. We worship success—in and out of the church. Those who are invited to speak in our colleges and churches are those who have succeeded in high-profile ventures. They are stars! No one ever invites a plumber or carpenter to come and speak to the congregation, college chapel, or youth group, even though that person may be the most Christlike, faithful Christian in the community. Why? Because there's no name recognition, no star power, no glitz. We listen instead to the athlete, entertainer, or business leader. We take from our culture the worship of celebrity. Certainly, I am not criticizing high-profile Christians, but the subtle message given is that you have to be successful in a material way to have something to say to the church or community. Success gives confirmation to the faith. So, if it is all about success, why even try things at which you cannot be a star? We fear failure, and we define failure as not finishing first or being the very best. Why try to pray faithfully, give generously, or live simply if there are others who are better at it? If you can't get an A—no, an A+—then don't even take the course. Such an attitude is sad when applied to high school or college course selection (as it often is), but it is devastating when it comes to our morning resolve to grow spiritually. We are called to be faithful, not perfect—remember this. I have come to believe that for many areas of our spiritual lives, we can grow by this: if it is worth being done, it is worth being done average. By this I mean that you don't have to finish first or be the best at tending your spiritual garden. Your only charge is to do *your* best. No comparisons requested and no fear of failure allowed.

And the knowledge of our lack of perfection, when accompanied by a view of God as a grouchy, mean, angry watchdog who just waits until we do something wrong to jump in and punish us, can lead to spiritual despair. If we're not perfect and God is just waiting for us to fail, then why even try? It's a fear that robs us of hope—and it is poor theology, too. Surely, the God who created us and loves us now is not sneaking around like a middle school principal trying to catch us smoking a cigarette, and then relishing in meting out our punishment. There is nothing we can do to make God stop loving us—nothing.

So, how do we deal with the fear of the unknown, the fear of failure, and the fear of an angry God? After we discuss fear's partner in anxiety—worry—we'll look at Scripture and offer some practical advice for doing so. Suffice it here to say that the fears we have discussed are real and not easily dismissed. The fundamental approach is not to deny that they exist, but simply to refuse to give in to them. In other words, honestly acknowledge them (be fierce with reality), recognize them for what they are, and move ahead anyway. Don't let them hold you back, distort reality, or rob you of hope. This, of course, is not a simple task, and there is no need to try it alone—but it can be done.

Worry

At some time or other, we have all been told to quit worrying. Just focus on what you can actually address, and let the rest go. Of course, we all agree but it is easier said than done. While we acknowledge that fear has both positive and negative aspects, not so with worry. At best, worry is simply a bad habit. When we worry about tomorrow, we end up carrying the burdens of the future along with the present. In effect, we needlessly carry a double load. Today has enough trials and tomorrow will come soon enough. There is no reward or prize for "worrying ahead." And we know that worry doesn't help make tomorrow any better, but it sure can take the energy and fun out of today! So, why do we worry so much, particularly if we know that worry doesn't help and can make things so much worse? For starters, it's free. You don't have to pay by the hour and you can do it anytime from anywhere. In addition, you can worry about anything—there's no limit! All this adds up to a free and easy habit. It's better than the Internet on Wi-Fi! And to top it off, worry is not understood in our culture to be as harmful as a "gossip" or "glutton" but it can be just as destructive to body and spirit. Jesus was quite clear in his Sermon on the Mount—don't worry. Just don't.

Often we worry about things totally beyond our control. We live in the "what-if" syndrome—what if this happens, what if it doesn't, what if she doesn't call, what if I don't get that job, what if, what if . . . . Worrying about things beyond our influence and control puts us in a helpless state. We become a victim, paralyzed by future maybes and possibilities. Constantly worrying about tomorrow doesn't help tomorrow, but it robs today of its joy and vitality. And worrying about tomorrow takes our attention away from that which we could be doing today. As such, it's a subtle from of procrastination, even spiritual laziness.

Sometimes we worry about things we bring upon ourselves. For example, many of us haven't learned to say no, so we overcommit. Then, we worry about how we're going to get everything done and what others will say or think about us if we don't. It's an unhealthy anxiety-producing cocktail. Life is much smoother when we maintain some personal boundaries and don't set ourselves up for stress and failure.

Ultimately, worry is a lack of trust. Surely, it is prudent to plan for the eventualities of life, but God isn't going to leave us or forsake us. That's a promise. We know that the darkness exists, but we can choose not to live in it. And we know that even a little bit of light can brighten up an entire room and illuminate the path. At the end of the day, worry is a tactile admission that we really don't trust God with what is beyond our control. The good news is that we do have a choice. We do not have to play the victim.

Scripture

It is clear from Scripture that anxiety is not good; it "weighs down the heart" (Prov 12:25). Instead of carrying this burden, we are instructed to "cast all your anxiety on him because he cares for you" (1 Pet 5:7). Give it to God because God cares for you. Let him do the heavy lifting. And again, "Do not be anxious about anything, but in every situation, by prayer and petition, with thanksgiving, present your requests to God" (Phil 4:6). Wow! Do not be anxious about *anything*. What a bold directive. How can we do this? Rather than be anxious, we are instructed to talk to God, ask, and be thankful—in *every* situation. The key, it seems to me, is to be thankful in our relationship with God for our relationship with God. And when we do, "the peace of God, which transcends all understanding, will guard your hearts and your minds in Christ Jesus" (Phil 4:7). Did you catch that? You won't be able to understand it or need to, but the peace of God will guard your . . . *mind*, too. What a wonderful promise.

Psalm 22 begins, "My God, my God, why have you forsaken me?" and Psalm 23 begins (this is much more familiar to all of us), "The Lord is my shepherd, I lack nothing." Interestingly, King David wrote both psalms. It is an apt description of life, isn't it? The road between Psalms 22 and 23 and back again is a road we've all traveled—and we still do. David was afraid at times, too, and when he was, he acknowledged it and talked to God about it. "When I am afraid, I put my trust in you" (Ps 56:3). He didn't let his fears (which were real) undermine his trust in God. That's a key. You see, there are certainly things that are stronger than fear. A few years ago, a small child fell into the deep end of a swimming pool in Memphis, Tennessee. His mother jumped into the pool and shoved him over to the edge of the pool and safety, but in doing so, she drowned. Now, I ask you: What in the world would make a grown person who had a real fear of water because she could not swim jump into the deep end of a swimming pool? Love, that's what. Love is much stronger than fear. That's why John writes, "There is no fear in love. But perfect love drives out fear" (1 John 4:18). When we put our trust in the one who loves us, we do not have to be controlled by fear.

When Jesus delivered what we now call the Sermon on the Mount (Matt 5–7), he had some things to say about worry, too—don't do it. "I tell you, do not be worried about your life . . . body, clothes" (Matt 6:25); "do not worry about tomorrow, for tomorrow will worry about itself" (Matt 6:34). Why? Because it just doesn't help. "Can any one of you by worrying add a single hour to our life?" Jesus asks (Matt 6:27). The answer is obvious—it doesn't help tomorrow, it only takes away from today. Don't do it.

Some Practical Advice

Before we conclude, let's talk about some practical steps you can take to deal with anxiety. First, understand that fear and worry will come. It is not productive to try to never worry, or to think that if you catch yourself worrying, you are a failure. No, trying not to think about something usually just increases your awareness of it. Instead, when you catch yourself being anxious, simply acknowledge it and focus your attention on something more productive. Just because something comes to mind doesn't mean that it has to control you. Stay in control.

Focus on doing the right thing or a good thing, not the perfect thing. You don't have to be perfect—we rarely are. If we prepare a meal for someone and it is not perfect, so what? It's really not a reflection on you. After all, did you prepare the meal just to receive a compliment, to demonstrate how perfect you are? If so, you'll be in a constant state of worry. You've set standards that you can't possibly live up to—or need to. Focus on doing good, not on being perfect. In the end, it's not really about you.

Also, remember that you don't have to believe everything you think. For example, you might be anxious about what others are thinking about you. Just because that particular worry comes to mind doesn't make it true. Most of the time, we don't need to be worried about what others are thinking about us—because the reality is that they're not. In other words, our worries don't necessarily reflect reality. It is much better to focus on the reality of God's love and faithfulness. That's a reality that you can count on.

Another strategy to keep in mind is that the best way out of anxiety is often to expose yourself to the things you are afraid of. Sometimes the only way forward is through. A motto from Upward Bound comes to mind, "If you can't get out of it, then get into it!" Just start slowly, and gradually things will become less ominous—and more comfortable, too. We don't always have control over what happens to us or how we feel about it, but we do get to choose how we respond to it.

Finally, sleep with bread. During World War II, thousands of children in London were left homeless as a result of the mass bombing raids. Even those who were rescued and moved to safe refuge found it difficult to sleep at night, worrying what tomorrow might bring. Those in charge came up with the idea of giving each child a piece of bread to sleep with at night. It was both symbolic and real—a tangible indication that there would be bread for tomorrow.[1] Why don't we all sleep with bread? Simply take some time each night before you sleep to think about the things for which you are most thankful, and about the parts of the day that gave you life and brought you love and renewal. Instead of worry and fear, let's sleep with those thoughts. Many have found this to be a life-giving way to end the day.

Conclusion

In this chapter, we have examined the reality and the consequences of anxiety for our spiritual development. In short, fear and worry rob us of our strength and intent. We focus on tomorrow at the expense of today, and we know that a steady diet of fear and worry about things we cannot control will leave us spiritually malnourished. In later sections of this book, we will look at a series of positive spiritual practices that will bring life to our spiritual gardens. Up to this point, we have been clearing out some bad weeds, discontent and anxiety. This is hard but necessary work, and there are a few more weeds to pull. Discouragement is next.

As we end this chapter on anxiety, let's embrace the wisdom of an old Appalachian saying, "Hope for the best, prepare for the worst, and be grateful for whatever happens." It sure beats worry.

Questions for Discussion and Reflection

1. In your life, where are the dragons? What situations do you most want to avoid?

2. What do you find yourself worrying about that is really beyond your control? What would be a helpful way to put that burden down?

1. See Dennis Linn, Sheila Fabricant Linn, and Matthew Linn, *Sleeping with Bread: Hold What Gives You Life* (Mahwah, NJ: Paulist Press, 1995).

3. What practical advice for dealing with anxiety did you find most helpful? Why?

4. If you began the practice of sleeping with bread, what would you say you were most thankful for in your life right now? What gives you life and renewal?

5. Do you ever think of God as a truant officer, someone who is out to catch and punish you because you're not perfect? Where does this image of God come from? Is there a better way to imagine and experience God?

I will try this day to live a simple, sincere, and serene life, repelling promptly every thought of discontent, anxiety . . .

— 3 —

Discouragement

Trouble has no necessary connection with discouragement. Discouragement has a germ of its own, as different from trouble as arthritis is different from a stiff joint.

—F. SCOTT FITZGERALD

Introduction

IF WE ARE TO take seriously our morning resolve to try each day to live a simple, sincere, and serene life, we know we will have to practice repelling promptly every thought of discontent (chapter 1) and anxiety (chapter 2). We need to add discouragement to the list. It is certainly no stranger to us, and although F. Scott Fitzgerald is correct—trouble has no necessary connection with discouragement—they are often intertwined in very deep ways. Why is it that troubles so often bring discouragement for some but not for others, and how can we repel promptly those thoughts of discouragement when they come our way? And why is it necessary to repel thoughts of discouragement in the first place? Isn't it just a part of the human condition? In this chapter, we'll look at discouragement more closely, distinguishing between losing heart, losing hope, and losing courage—all components of discouragement. Then, we'll visit a story from the Bible that illustrates the demotivating nature of discouragement and its negative impact on spiritual growth. We'll conclude with some practical advice about how to manage and ultimately repel every thought of discouragement.

Along the way, I'll point to the faithful character of God, a promise and reality that we can depend on as we work to clear our spiritual gardens of yet another pernicious weed.

Losing Heart

We are a culture of winners and losers, perhaps one of the most competitive societies on the face of the earth. Of course, there are some positive aspects to being competitive. You work harder and push yourself to do your very best, our economy is based on persons and organizations competing at a high level, and we accomplish things that were heretofore unimagined— think of the Internet and the trip to the moon to name just two. But framing your life around winning and losing has a dark side, too, and it can impact all of us if we are not careful. If we let losing a game or a promotion or a job take away our sense of worth and well-being—our spirit, our confidence, our way, then we are truly diminished spiritually. It is certainly a great test of courage to encounter failure or defeat without losing head or heart, but I would like to suggest that there is even a greater test of courage—the courage to step back (or out) and not get caught up in the first place in the race for appearance, affluence, and achievement that is so central to self-worth in our culture (and in our churches, too). In other words, simply don't play the winner-loser game, but instead participate in God's economy where we, all of us, are of infinite worth, and where collaboration and commitment are the higher values. Let's start by refusing to play the win/lose game, denying its power over our lives. We are called to live in a different kingdom.

Discouragement is insidious because it robs us of our motivation, and our words give us away. "I can't . . . That won't work . . . What if . . . The problem with that is . . . It's no use . . ." Always a problem, never a possibility. Have you ever had to spend a day, even an hour or two, with someone who can see the problem with everything and the possibility with nothing? They not only see the glass half empty, they also suspect that someone has poisoned what remains. It honestly takes away your spirit, doesn't it? Just think what it must do to their spirit. When you let discouragement linger and dominate your language, it kills your spirit—and the spirits of those around you. Your motivation dries up as you wallow in the mud. Sadly, it is a learned behavior. The good news is that with work and intention, it can be unlearned. It can be repelled promptly.

Losing Hope

Discouragement not only diminishes your spirit and motivation, it chokes out confidence, too. In short, you lose hope. Of course, some losses are actually helpful. For example, if you become disillusioned, in that you lose your illusions, that can be a good thing. Sometimes we expect far more from a trip, a relationship, a job, or an experience than can possibly be realized. When we carry misconceptions, things that cannot be achieved, our alignment with reality is off and we can become discouraged and lose hope. If you can examine and challenge those unrealistic expectations, they can be modified; but you have to be honest with yourself. This is hard to do. Often it takes a good friend or listening ear to help you work through those things that discourage you. Remember, when you've set yourself up for failure, there's only one person at fault.

We also lose hope because we want everything now. We are an impatient lot, aren't we? We eat fast food, watch on-demand movies, check our phones every three minutes for a message, buy everything on credit, and want the big job promotion today! We can easily lose our sense of seasons, the knowledge that growth takes time. Sometimes when nothing seems to be happening, something is happening. If you break your arm and wear a cast, it seems like nothing is happening. Oh, how you want the cast off now. But underneath, things are happening—the break is healing and your bones are becoming stronger. You can't hurry the process though, or there will be a setback. Healing takes time, and so does spiritual growth. As an old proverb cautions: Every seed knows its time—all in good time. Waiting can be difficult. We even get discouraged when others don't instantly see the spiritual growth and changes we are making in our lives. Patience is such a positive virtue because it fends off discouragement; it nurtures hope. If we race through life wanting and expecting everything now, we not only invite discouragement, we miss the joy of the journey and many spiritual lessons along the way.

The theologian Jürgen Moltmann makes an interesting and crucial distinction between optimism and hope.[1] Both are good things. For Moltmann, optimism is faith in progress based on past events. That is to say, we look at what has happened and project it out to the future. If the rains stops in Oregon each July and has done so for the past twelve summers, we can be optimistic that it will stop raining again next July, too. We have faith in what

1. See *Theology of Hope* (Minneapolis: Fortress, 1993).

we can predict. On the other hand, hope is faith in the character and trustworthiness of God, who can transform any situation and bring about something entirely new, even astonishing. It becomes truly an adventure. Think of the Advent—something no one could have possibly predicted given the events of the previous year. God wrought something new, and invited us to join in the ultimate adventure, an adventure of faith, Advent. When we are discouraged, we don't have to be bound by what has happened in our past. It doesn't have to determine our future. We can place our hope and trust in the God who is with us, who is patiently working to transform our lives, inviting us on an adventure with him. Hope brings confidence.

Losing Courage

As the word suggests, sometimes discouragement means that we literally lack or have lost courage. So often, it is not that we lack the ability to move forward and make changes, but we lack the courage to do so. There are those who can somehow move forward in the face of tragedy and trouble, but most of us struggle mightily. For all of us, discouragement is a bad weed because it brings with it a certain lack of initiative and motivation. We get stuck in a circle dance of inaction.

Perhaps some of us have more innate resolve than others, but we all need encouragement from time to time. Living without any encouragement will slowly and surely dry up your spirit. The good news is that giving encouragement costs nothing and means everything. Sadly, though, it is a rare spiritual practice. I will have more to say about encouragement later in this chapter, so suffice it to say here that perhaps one of the best ways to dispel discouragement promptly is to prayerfully, consciously, and persistently be an encourager, to give courage to others. As is often the case, we grow spiritually when we focus on the needs of others. Perhaps the best way to gain courage is to give it away.

Scripture

Before we turn to some practical advice for dealing promptly with discouragement, I want us to look at two stories from Scripture that deal with different aspects of discouragement—one from the New Testament (losing heart and hope) and one from the Old Testament (finding courage). First, the New Testament story: The Healing at the Pool (John 5:1–15). As Jesus was walking by the pool of Bethesda near the Sheep Gate in Jerusalem, a pool that was reputed to have healing power when it stirred—but only for the first one in the pool—he learned that an invalid had been laying by the pool for thirty-eight years. And there were many other blind, lame, and infirm waiting there, too. Jesus asked him if he wanted to get well. What a question to a man who had waited all that time. Of course, he wanted to get well! But listen to his answer—"I can't. I don't have anyone to help me into the water. Someone always beats me to the pool." Jesus, the Son of God, asks him if he wants to get well, and he answers, "I can't!" It is a response fostered by years of disappointment. Rather than shouting "Yes!" he started giving all the reasons why it wouldn't work and what had gone wrong in the past. He had been doing the same thing for thirty-eight years with the same result. Insanity has been defined as doing the same thing over and over again, but expecting different results. I'm not saying that the invalid at the pool was insane, but his strategy for healing surely was. Thirty-eight years of disappointment should have taught him that. When asked if he wanted to be healed, it was the language of discouragement that spoke—"I can't. It won't work. I've already tried." Fortunately for the invalid (and for us), Jesus did not listen to the voice of discouragement. He knew that discouragement robs us of our heart and hope, and he healed him on the spot. I wonder how often in our own discouragement we miss opportunities that are staring us right in the face. Far too often, I fear. That's why we can't let thoughts of discouragement linger. They can spread like a bad weed, and choke out heart, hope, and initiative.

One of my favorite verses in the Bible is 1 Chronicles 11:22: "Benaiah . . . went down into a pit on a snowy day and killed a lion." Now, I don't ever want to fight a lion—particularly with only a sword and spear. No, thank you! But if I did, it certainly wouldn't be in a pit with a very limited number of exits. And if I had to fight a lion in a pit, it wouldn't be on a snowy day with poor footing. That's sounds like a prescription for disaster to me. So, why did Benaiah go into a pit on a snowy day to fight a lion? There is no indication that he was crazy or some type of thrill seeker. I think he was very nervous—even afraid—but he went anyway. Why? Because it was his job to fight lions, and that's where the lion was. He didn't let his very real fears keep him from leaning into the task at hand. Being courageous doesn't mean that there is no fear. Rather, it means that fear is not in control. Is it any wonder that King David, when he needed someone he could count on to escort his son, Solomon, to the place where he would be anointed as the next king, called on Benaiah for the task? He had reliable courage.

In the first story, we see how debilitating the language of discouragement can be. Sometimes we get locked into such despair that we can't even recognize help when it is standing right in front of us. In the second story, we see that fear and the lack of courage are not the same thing. We need to acknowledge our fears, but not let them determine our actions. Before we close this chapter, I want to offer several practical ways for dealing with discouragement.

Some Practical Advice

At some point or another, we all travel through the land of disappointment. It's inevitable. Here are four very practical ways to deal with discouragement when it raises its ugly head. One key is to not get stuck in the mud. In other words, don't just stand there—keep walking! When discouragement comes, acknowledge it but don't let it take your heart and hope. Resolve to make the journey with faith in God, and trust him to be with you. As strange as it may sound at the time, it can be an adventure. There is faith and spiritual growth to be had. Look forward, not back, and keep moving. Be still, but not frozen in place.

Second, remember that you don't have to make the journey alone—and you probably shouldn't. Sharing with someone is a way to gain and keep perspective. It is extremely helpful to have a trusted friend or counselor who will honestly point out when your thinking and actions go sideways. When you start to play the "I can't" or "The problem with that is" card, you need a good friend who will say, "Stop. That's just not helpful." You can ask for help in finding alternative ways to think about the situation, and then listen. Don't play the victim.

Third, be patient. Don't lose heart because things do not happen in your preferred timetable. Be careful to distinguish between something that is not working, and something that is not happening when you want it to. You can't plant in May and harvest in June. There is a seasonal rhythm to life that can't be forced. Good things usually take time. And we have no promise that everything we undertake will be successful the first time anyway, if ever. Failure need not lead to discouragement. Learn from your mistakes and try again. Not every seed that you plant will flourish. That's part of the seasonal rhythm of life, too. Be patient.

Finally, spend time around folk who are natural encouragers, those who lift the human spirit. You know who they are. Their optimism is contagious, and it is fun to be with them. And to the extent possible, avoid the negativity of persons who speak the language of discouragement. If you are working to dispel promptly every thought of discouragement, their approach will not be helpful. Choose to be with persons that you want to be like. And intentionally choose to become an encourager to others. Commit to encourage at least three persons each day. Sometimes this spiritual practice is called speaking words of benediction. The next time you and a friend or co-worker are parting, look them directly in the eyes, tell them what you appreciate about them, and how you will pray for them. When you focus on others and speak words of encouragement, something good takes root in your own life, too. That's a kingdom reality.

Conclusion

In this chapter, we examined in turn three aspects of discouragement that hinder spiritual growth: losing heart, losing hope, and losing courage. We then looked at two stories from Scripture that gave insight into the language of discouragement and its impact on our spiritual resolve, and the relationship between fear and courage. As it turns out, you can have both. Finally, four practical words of advice were offered: don't get stuck in the mud, don't go it alone, be patient, and be an encourager every day. When tough times come, discouragement does not have to be the result unless you choose to make it so. Ultimately, if we put our trust in the character and promises of God to work in and through all that we face, and in us, too, we are invited to participate in a great spiritual adventure with God. What could be better than that!

Questions for Reflection and Discussion

1. Do you have a close friend or "listening ear" who will walk with you faithfully and respond to you truthfully? If so, do you honestly listen to them? If not, where might you find one?

2. Where in your life are you most competitive—to a fault? Does it ever lead to discouragement?

3. What things do you find most difficult to wait for? Why do you think waiting is so difficult for you?

4. Think of the last time someone spoke words of encouragement (or a benediction) to you. How did it make you feel?

5. Who is the best encourager you know? How could you be more like that person?

I will try this day to live a simple, sincere, and serene life, repelling promptly every thought of discontent, anxiety, discouragement . . .

— 4 —

Impurity

In the story of the Prodigal Son, the father does not send the son for a bath before hugging him.

—*DALLAS WILLARD*

Introduction

A CHAPTER ON IMPURITY—YIKES! Discontent, anxiety, and discouragement are easy to talk about, but impurity—my impurity? Yes, we need to pull that weed, too—as it turns out, it is an entire bunch of weeds. For each of us, the bunch is a bit different. We're not going to talk about sexual impurity, not because it isn't destructive (which it is) but rather because so much attention and writing have been focused on it in our culture and our churches that there is little I can add to the conversation. Instead, we are going to address some all-to-common forms of impurity that rob us of our spiritual growth: gossip, unkindness, and greed. They are truly devastating, but they are too often dismissed as just bad habits or poor behavior. In doing so, we let these plants grow in our spiritual gardens, thinking that they aren't all that harmful. Sadly, at harvest time, we see that not only did they bear bitter fruit; they choked out other growth, too. This result is avoidable if we promptly dispel these thoughts—that is, deal with them when they first crop up. In this chapter, we will discuss these impurities frankly; look to see what Jesus had to say about them in the Sermon on the Mount; and offer some practical advice for dealing with impurity as we try each day to live a simple, sincere, and serene life.

Misconceptions about Impurity

Let's start by identifying two powerful misconceptions about impurity. The first misconception is that *purity means perfection*. It is not helpful because it implies that we are pure only if we are perfect. It suffers from something philosophers call dualism: the idea that only opposites exist—right/wrong, good/evil, win/lose, love/hate, and pure/impure—with no middle ground. There are only two states, and the one excludes the other. If we think about purity in this way and we know that we are not perfect, then purity is unachievable. We walk around with a deep sense of shame and failure, feeling that we must be unacceptable to God. Such feelings are devastating to spiritual growth. It is more helpful to think about impurity as existing on a continuum, say on a sliding scale from one to ten. At one time, you may be a three; at other time, an eight. If we think about working on impurity as moving up the scale as opposed to becoming perfect (being a ten all the time), it makes the work of dealing with impurity both possible and plausible.

The second misconception is that *purity means keeping all the rules*. Of course, there is a long tradition of rule keeping in religious circles. We know that the Pharisees were rule keepers, and somewhere along the line, the rules became more important than relationships—even with God. In fact, keeping all the rules became the way that faith was properly expressed and membership determined. It became a house of rules. To be pure meant to keep all the rules. Sadly, this is not something exclusive to biblical times; we see this in our churches, too. We make up rules for just about everything. Some are helpful, no doubt; others are just silly. But when purity comes to mean that we keep all the rules, we're in trouble. Although we go through the motions, we lose heart. That's no way to become more like Christ. Jesus was clear in the Sermon on the Mount that our righteousness does not come from keeping rules, but from what we say and do—in both word and deed. The greatest commandment we have is to love God and our neighbors as ourselves, not to keep rules and regulations. Let's look at three common impure behaviors in word and deed.

Gossip

Gossip is a particularly widespread practice. At some point or another, most of us engage in it. Even though we agree that it is not helpful, why is it so prevalent and so delightful to engage in? I think it's because in some strange way, gossip makes us feel better about ourselves, superior with regard to others. The truth is, however, that it is a dangerous and hurtful practice, often to the person being spoken of, and always to the person doing the gossiping. My grandmother would have nothing to do with gossip. She always told me that it is good to live as though the neighbors were watching and the windows were wide open. That's good advice. I call it the six o'clock news test. What if we acted as if all our conversations were going to appear on the local six o'clock news? How would that change our talk? Would we be proud or ashamed? What if we used the six o'clock news test to temper what we say about others? What if we concentrated on saying only good things about other folk? Wouldn't that be an affirming and helpful spiritual practice? What would happen if we started good news circles instead of using the church prayer chain to spread rumors? It might be quiet for a bit, but I suspect that we would all get the hang of it. Even though bad news travels quickly, perhaps we can give good news roots and wings.

Gossip simply reveals your character. The Bible is clear that the words that come out of your mouth are an indication of what is in your heart. And gossip does not need to be false to be evil. There is a lot of truth that need not be repeated. Gossip is destructive to community, hurtful to reputations and relationships, and dangerous to the listener, too. We should be wary of the gossiper. After all, if someone will gossip to you, they most surely will gossip about you. You can count on it; gossip is no respecter of persons.

It is important to develop the practice of repelling quickly every thought (and act) of gossip. It takes diligence, perception, and courage. It starts by learning, as my mother used to say, to zip your lip. In other words, start by simply committing to avoid gossip. Just don't do it. If you start, then zip your lip or bite your tongue. Stop! And if someone starts to gossip to you, just hold up your hand—palm out, and say, "Please stop." Move the conversation to a positive note. When I encounter gossip, I try to quickly interject, "Here's what I like about . . .". Statements of this kind usually redirect the conversation. And if they don't, then I simply walk away. Don't give support to a wrongful conversation by saying nothing. This is really easy to do. While we would never gossip, we do listen in and say nothing—only to repeat the "news" later. In doing so, we become complicit.

In the last analysis, we cannot stop others from gossiping. I wish we could. We do not, however, have to let this impurity taint us. We can consistently acknowledge that gossip is harmful and resolve to be positive, building others up and not tearing them down. We can carefully watch what we say and monitor what we hear—and we can think the best of others. That's a spiritual choice that is ours to make. We can refuse to let that weed take over our spiritual garden, knowing that if given even half a chance, it will.

Unkindness

I don't have to make the case that unkindness is hurtful. We know it is. Not only is unkindness insensitive, it is toxic, too. Few acts poison a healthy relationship, organization, or community faster or more completely, and curiously, those who are unkind are often oblivious to how hurtful their actions really are. They just don't get it, or even worse, they don't care. Over the years, I've come to believe that there are two warning signs that indicate that unkindness or meanness may be lurking in the shadows: unkindness accompanies those who can't laugh at themselves, and those who love to be first. Meanness is a perverse way of preserving a high view of self or the expectation that high respect and regard are owed, not earned. I will have more to say about self-seeking in the next chapter, so suffice it here to say that when we try to protect the idea that we are perfect and deserve the seat of honor, bad things happen. The sad trilogy of jealousy, meanness, and malice follows like a tedious argument, and people get hurt.

Okay, that's enough about others; let's talk about us. How do we deal with unkindness in our own lives? It's easy to see and condemn unkindness "out there"—but what about "in here," in our own spiritual garden? First, let's be honest enough to admit that we can be unkind, too, and when we are, let's be sensitive enough to recognize what we have done and humble enough to apologize and ask for forgiveness. When this weed crops up, pull it out right away. Don't rationalize it away or let it take root by ignoring it.

Second, we are responsible for what we do, even if it is a response or reaction to what others have done to us. Turning the other cheek and returning good for evil are not easy things to do, but we are told to do it anyway. As my mother would say to me, "One bad turn does not excuse another, and two wrongs never make a right." She was correct, of course, even though returning evil for evil is very tempting at times. The satisfaction for doing so is short lived, though, and the harm that is done demeans our own spirit in profound ways—often for a very long time.

Finally, as simplistic as it sounds, the best antidote for unkindness is kindness. And kindness is even more powerful when it comes totally unexpected, out of the blue. It may be one of the most powerful ways to bring about transformations in persons, organizations, or communities. Unexpected kindness, now there's a grace-filled response to meanness. And it is important to remember that kindness is a choice, and we always have a choice. We can't control what happens to us, but we can control our reactions—and our actions.

It is a spiritual principle that being kind not only impacts others (which it does), it changes you, too. It is yet another example of how God works in every situation, even in the hurtful ones. Simply put, it is an important part of the process of learning to live a simple, sincere, and serene life. Of course, there are a few other things that are important, too, but I think you get the point. Kindness is a formative spiritual act, and being kind is a rich and generous way to live.

Greed

When Michael Douglas, playing the high-flying, fast-dealing stockbroker Gordon Gekko, the lead character in the 1987 film *Wall Street*, uttered those magic words, "Greed, for lack of a better word, is good," he touched a raw nerve. Although it sounded stark and heartless, it was an expression of what we have come to value and practice in our culture. For many, greed is good, and someone (albeit a movie character) finally said it out loud. How could this be? How could greed come to be thought of as a good thing?

Of course, there are many factors at work to make greed acceptable, but let's talk about one that hits very close to home—conspicuous consumption. Thorstein Veblen coined this term in 1899. Conspicuous consumption refers to the competitive and extravagant consumption practices and leisure activities that aim to indicate membership in a superior social class. Now, most of us are put off by the idea that buying and having things would be an indication of our social class, but just take a look at the automobile ads on TV these days. The more expensive the car you drive, the better person you are—especially in a culture where the highest values are the three A's: appearance, achievement, and affluence. In short, we are told that your prestige and power are determined in large part by your possessions—your house(s), cars, yachts, memberships, clothes, and jewelry. The more you have, the higher the prestige, so the arms race is on. You simply can't have too many expensive things, so greed is good if it gets you more stuff.

Now, it is easy to point out and criticize extravagant examples of conspicuous consumption. Honestly, who needs to carry a handbag that costs $8,000? The answer is someone who can afford it. Rather than being embarrassed by such a silly display of wealth in a starving world, it is actually a symbol of prestige in our society. If we were honest, many of us would buy one too if we could afford to do so. While the level of spending is not the same, greed and conspicuous consumption are prevalent in our churches and neighborhoods, too. How many of us feel better about ourselves with a new car or new clothes? How many of us, when we are down, go shopping? In our society, there is a direct connection between buying things and feeling good about ourselves. In such an environment, is it any wonder that greed is good—or at least understandable?

While prevalent today, certainly greed was not invented in 1899. History is full of examples. Napoleon sarcastically observed that he was surrounded by priests who repeated incessantly that their kingdom was not of this world, and yet worked diligently to get all the possessions they could get. Sadly, we do the same thing. One reason for this behavior is that we all have trouble differentiating between wants and needs—what we want and what we really need. Our culture is good at converting wants into needs, and that plays on greed. It is important to consider the values of God's economy. He is the Enough God—he will supply all your needs (Phil 4:19)—that's enough. On the other hand, greed is never satisfied, an endless chain of attempts to achieve satisfaction. The trouble is, it (whatever "it" is) is never enough. I think I like God's economy better.

So, with all the social pressure to get and display things, how can we promptly repel thoughts about getting and spending—eliminating greed? The antidote is found in giving: giving thanks, giving back, and giving credit. No matter how bad things are in your life, you can wake up each day and be thankful for what you do have. There are far too many in this world who are desperate for a simple meal and a safe place to sleep. Most of us have more than we can ever use. Some churches and fellowships are beginning to intentionally cut their possessions in half and give them away—as a tangible practice of giving thanks. Think about it. Most of us could weed out half of our closets, give the clothes away, and get by just fine. Living with more gratitude and less things. Isn't that a wonderful expression of anti-greed? The best things in life, as it turns out, aren't things at all.

Rather than working to get more and more, let's put the emphasis on giving back and paying forward. We will pass on that which we have received, expecting nothing in return. I believe being an anonymous donor is an authentic virtue—and hard to do because we all want to be *known* as kind and generous. That is, we all have egos, but they don't have to rule our actions. Let's give and expect nothing in return, and if someone finds out that you're the giver, just tell him or her to pay it forward—give to someone else when they can. We all know of individuals in our own communities who quietly do good things with no self-centered motives or desire for recognition. Let's join them and be counted among that group. We often think that we make a living in order to have things. Maybe so, but we make a life by giving things away. Let's be givers.

Yet another way to combat greed is to give credit where credit is due. It is truly a greedy act to think or claim that you did it all by yourself. In whatever endeavor we undertake and successfully complete, there are always others who believed in us, invested in us, supported us, and saw more in us than we saw in ourselves. We always stand on the shoulders of others. I remind graduating students that it is perfectly fine to celebrate such a huge achievement, but please don't ever forget to stop and say, "Thank you." Graduation isn't just about you. Sharing the limelight or credit is not just a generous thing to do; it is a spiritual obligation, too.

Scripture

It is easy to find biblical references condemning gossip, meanness, greed, and other common forms of impurity. In fact, admonitions against impurity and stories telling of the results of such behaviors run from Genesis to Revelation. Simply put, it is not a good thing. The message is simple, "Stop; stay away; don't do that!" Rather than a sweeping review of Scripture, however, let's look specifically at one passage in 3 John that insightfully reveals the destructive results of one form of impurity—loving to be first. In a short note to Gaius, John the Elder writes: "I wrote to the church, but Diotrephes, who loves to be first, will not welcome us. So when I come, I will call attention to what he is doing, spreading malicious nonsense about us. Not satisfied with that, he even refuses to welcome other believers. He also stops those who want to do so and puts them out of the church" (3 John

9–10). What a legacy: incivility, malicious gossip, inhospitality, coerciveness, and exclusivity. Here we see some of the destructive behaviors that accompany loving to be first. Of course, it is nice to be first—at least at most things. But loving to be first, needing to be first, doing anything it takes to be first—that's impurity in action!

Note that Diotrephes (who loves to be first) did not welcome the correction of others. You see, when someone loves to be first, there isn't any room for other opinions. After all, if you are the best, contrary suggestions and advice are not needed. In fact, they are unwelcome. At best, such advice will be ignored, but usually there is a stronger reaction. The advice is unwelcome, and the messengers are talked about, too—malicious gossip takes center stage. That's what gossip does—it gives the gossiper a false sense of superiority at the expense of another person. When you love to be first, dealing with others who won't worship you is difficult. It seems good to ignore them, and if they won't go away, then disparage them. This is what Diotrephes did to John and his party.

Sadly, there's more. When you love to be first, you not only treat others rudely and gossip about them, you also push them out—making them invisible. They are not welcome in your circle, the inner circle. And as we see in the actions of Diotrephes, he not only pushed John's group away, he coerced others to do the same. What a sad litany of impurity. In the end, it is the one who loves to be first who is demeaned, but many others are hurt in the process.

It is only fair to note that this is not just a New Testament phenomenon. In our communities, schools, and churches, there are those who love to be first, and will do just about anything to maintain their high status. This, of course, is dangerous. And we all fall into this trap from time to time. Our culture promotes competition and we worship winners—those who finish first. It is a sobering reminder that Jesus taught that kingdom values are vastly different: the first shall be last, and anyone who wants to lead must be the servant of all (Matt 20:26). We might even have to wash some feet from time to time. In fact, we are told to do so.

Some Practical Advice

To deal honestly and carefully with our own impurity is a difficult but necessary task if we earnestly seek to see our spiritual gardens grow. These bad weeds have to go if new growth is to flourish, but how? First, don't think or act like you're perfect. No one is—not even you and me. In essence, we are all broken. We know this, but we rarely talk about it, even in church—perhaps especially in church. Instead, we all show up on Sunday mornings looking good and on our best behavior as if we were on some sort of job interview. Wouldn't it be wonderful to be part of a church that carefully practiced redemptive remorse instead of shooting the wounded? I think so. The best way to start dealing with impurity is to be real, honestly and openly confessing that we are not always at our best. The good news is that grace and forgiveness abound for all of us.

The second word of advice is to make no excuses. There are three classic excuses for behaving badly. The first is denial—"That wasn't really me. I wasn't myself today." Of course, this begs the question: Then who were you and who did this? The truth of the matter is that it was you, but it takes courage to admit it. The second classic excuse is explanation—"That's just the way I am. It's my character. I was brought up that way. I can't help the way I act." Of course, explaining who you are and how you got here does not excuse your behavior or absolve you from making Godly choices now. Living in bondage to the past is a choice we often make. The third classic excuse is rationalization—"Well, they did it to me. They deserve it. Besides, everyone does it." When we hear these excuses, we smile. But we all use them, don't we? My mother would ask me: "If everyone jumped off the bridge, would you jump, too?" The truth is that sometimes I probably would. Peer pressure is so very difficult to manage, and it doesn't necessarily get easier with age. Rather than making excuses, a much better approach is to simply say, "Yes, that's me, and I'm sorry. Please forgive me."

The third word of advice is this: don't make impurity a habit Of course, there are times when we all do things that we know that we shouldn't, but to return to that behavior again and again shapes us in very destructive ways. We do have choices. If you honestly know that you struggle with some form of impurity, think carefully and avoid those situations where that habit or behavior is accepted or allowable. In other words, if you want to diet, it's best to avoid afternoons in a bakery. Don't dwell there.

Finally, spend your time with persons that you want to be like. The more time you spend with folk, the more you will become like them. That's the general rule. So, choose to spend time with those who make you better. Menander, the famous Greek poet, wrote that knowing yourself is a good thing, but in many cases knowing others is even better. So, watch the company you keep. And the New Testament quotes Menander this way, "Bad company corrupts good character" (1 Cor 15:33). Translation: don't spend your time with bad company.

Conclusion

In this chapter, we took a hard look at impurity—not our favorite subject because we're all broken in some way. In particular, we examined gossip, unkindness, and greed. Then, we examined a short passage from 3 John, looking at Diotrephes—who loved to be first—and the negative spiral of behaviors that often accompany this commonplace form of impurity: incivility, malicious gossip, inhospitality, coerciveness, and exclusivity. We ended the chapter by offering four words of advice for dealing with impurity: don't think or act like you're perfect, don't make excuses, don't make impurity a habit, and surround yourself with good role models. Most of us become much like the persons we hang with.

The good news for all of us is that although we're broken pots—we're not perfect—God loves and cares for us just as we are. Remember the story of the Prodigal Son (which is really a story about his father, our father). Obviously, the son was not perfect, far from it. In fact, he was tired, embarrassed, ashamed, and dirty—and he smelled awful, too. So, what did the father do? He ran to him, gave him a hug, welcomed him home, and threw a party. Grace came running and hugging! God wants to do the same for each of us, too.

Questions for Discussion and Reflection

1. When is admitting that you're not perfect most difficult for you? Why do you think you expect so much from yourself in these situations?

2. Be honest, when you talk about others, what is the payoff for doing so? What would be a good strategy for you to stay in positive territory when you encounter gossip?

3. Think of a time when you came up short—your actions proved to be less than kind? How did you respond? How could it have been different?

4. In what area of your life is the desire or need to be first problematic for you? How can you deal with this desire in an effective manner?

5. Who would be a good role model for you as you seek to grow spiritually? How could you spend more time with that person or community?

*I will try this day to live a simple, sincere, and serene life,
repelling promptly every thought of discontent, anxiety, discouragement, impurity . . .*

— 5 —

Self-Seeking

Love is patient, love is kind. It does not envy, it does not boast, it is not proud. It is not rude, it is not self-seeking . . .

—*1 CORINTHIANS 13:4–5A*

Introduction

BEFORE WE TAKE A fresh look at cultivating some positive spiritual practices and helpful attitudes in Part II—cheerfulness, magnanimity, charity, and the habit of holy silence—we need to pull one more noxious weed, self-seeking. This is a tough one because there is such a fine line between self-esteem and self-seeking. The first is beneficial; the latter, not so much. In fact, it can be downright harmful. The American writer, John Jay Chapman, wondered if there is something in business that "desiccates and flattens out" folk and turns them "into dried leaves at the age of forty," presumably because he saw so many who were. It wasn't their work, he observed, but rather the intensity of their self-seeking that ruined them.[1] And incessant self-seeking not only turns one's spirit into a dried leaf, it flattens out others, too. Much like secondhand smoke, self-seeking steals the spirits of those around you. Think how you feel after spending time with someone who can only talk about himself or herself. You come away empty—your spirit is dried out like an old leaf. If we truly want to grow spiritually, self-seeking has to go. In this chapter, we'll look at several modes of self-promotion, see

1. John Jay Chapman, *Practical Agitation*. (London: Forgotten, 2013), 56–57.

PART I—REPELLING NEGATIVITY

what Scripture has to say about self-seeking, and then discuss several ways to keep self and neighbor in proper balance.

Modes of Self-Promotion

Boasting

Boasting and bragging are often used in exchange, meaning the same thing. I like to use this subtle but helpful distinction. For me, boasting is self-promotion about what you have done, while bragging is self-promotion about what you are doing. Let me explain. Boasting is the result of excessive pride and self-satisfaction about achievements, positions, and connections. Have you ever been with someone who can top you at anything? If you've read a good book, she's read five and personally knows all the authors. If you've been to Paris, he's been there eight times—twice at the invitation of the French President. If you mention the local priest, she knows the bishop. If you are to be honored by your local church, out of humility he's already turned down the regional award. You simply can't win; in fact, you can't even stay in the game! Here's the good news. It *is* a game, and you *don't* have to play it—nor should you. Boasting is ultimately a desperate attempt to prop up an ailing ego, and it edifies neither the boaster nor the listener. If such boasting involves exaggerations, then it is deceitful, too. And even if the facts are true, it is not helpful. It is a persistent wind that dries out your spirit.

Bragging

On the other hand, bragging is the fatiguing work of bringing attention to your present activities—look what I am doing! Of course, the focus is on the word "I" and the implied message is, "I am wonderful and you are not so much." At the university where I teach, there are professors who simply cannot help but promote themselves and their work, letting everyone know what they have published, where they have been invited to speak, what recognitions they have received, who they are emailing, and how wonderful their students think they are in the classroom. Honestly, it is a very subtle and arrogant form of incivility. They don't even notice that they have colleagues. And, of course, it is not only at the university where such bragging goes on. The church is just as vulnerable, perhaps even more so. Why does our culture give permission for us to promote ourselves so relentlessly?

Think of all the time and attention that goes into boasting and bragging. Honestly, the incessant self-focus of social media keeps me away most days. What if that same energy was used to build others up, to encourage colleagues and promote their good work? Wouldn't that be wonderful? When we continually brag about ourselves (or our kids), we forfeit the opportunity to listen to others and speak into their lives. What a sad loss this is. We are significantly diminished by our own actions.

Self-Importance

Another mode of self-promotion is building up your own sense of importance by making sure that others know all that you have. Your behavior screams, look at me! In the last chapter, we discussed the repellent nature of conspicuous consumption that is so .prevalent in our society—the encouragement to display wealth because it makes you feel better about yourself and others think more highly of you (or so you assume). Certainly, commercials for high-end products like automobiles and jewelry reinforce this behavior by defining luxury in terms of good feelings. Owning this phone or that car will make you feel good about yourself, and others feel good about you, too. The not-so-subtle message is that if you don't buy and prominently display their product, you are somehow diminished as a person in important ways. This is so very sad. Of course, this is unnecessary and misguided, but honestly it is not simply about the purchase and display of things to feel better. If it were, it would be easy to address—just hide the credit cards. Unfortunately, we also attempt to derive some of our self-importance from our abilities, our opportunities, our family histories, our memberships, even our opportunities. We can take almost any aspect of our lives and use it in selfish and thoughtless ways to make us feel better or look superior, needlessly promoting ourselves. When we do, it becomes a mode of self-seeking.

Self-Centered

It's hard to work with someone when the agenda is always about them. They need the best office, the most convenient work schedule, the first vacation choice, the best hotels, business-class tickets, the best territory, the top of the conference program, and a seat at the head table. It is a circle of self-centered behavior that is sad to see and wearisome to experience. When I

41

first joined the management team of a bank in Kansas City, the president of the bank took me into the money vault and told me to look at the cash on hand—about $250,000. He told me that I would be a great bank official as long as I remembered that it wasn't my money. It belonged to someone else. It was a lesson that I have never forgotten. How often do we forget that it isn't our office, our unit, our administrative assistant, our travel funds, or our parish? They don't belong to us; they belong to God. I don't mean to be simplistic here, but in reality they really do. What if we approached our work, community, or church with no self-serving expectation of ownership? What if, instead, with grateful hearts, we understood our work to be God-given opportunities? It could be the spiritual difference between having a flourishing garden and becoming a dried-out leaf at forty.

Another aspect of self-centered behavior is the orientation that everything has to have something in it for me. If fact, you often hear that very question: What's in it for me? (Sometimes this is asked in a less direct manner, perhaps, but the same question nonetheless.) And we all know of persons who will not participate without getting something in return—a meal, a door prize, a tribute, or some other form of recognition. Again, the issue is the compulsion to place one's self at the very heart of every conversation, activity, relationship, or worship experience. Balance is lost and the center cannot hold.

Scripture

Before offering some practical words of advice for repelling promptly every thought of self-seeking, let's look at a very familiar passage in Scripture from the Sermon on the Mount. In Matthew, Jesus is quite clear that giving, praying, and fasting are to be done with great care. "Be careful not to practice your righteousness in front of others to be seen by them" (Matt 6:1). Certainly, they are good things. In fact, we are going to spend a good deal of time in coming chapters discussing the value of generosity, prayer, and fasting as formative spiritual practices. They strengthen us and help our neighbors. We should give, pray, and fast, so why the caution? Is it possible that truly good things, even formative spiritual practices, can become toxic in some way?

Of course, the answer is yes. Good things can become an empty practice, or even worse, a means of self-seeking. Clearly, Jesus is focusing on the heart of the doer rather than on the value of the practices themselves.

Is Jesus suggesting that we shouldn't be generous? No, but he does say, "So when you give to the needy, do not announce it with trumpets, as the hypocrites do in the synagogues and on the streets" (Matt 6:2–3). When done publically, giving can easily become more about the giver than about the gift. Sadly, the giver becomes the center of attention. When this happens, humility is missing and giving is cheapened. And the attention received is like the icing on the cake. It is certainly sweet. But if giving is done with this intent, Jesus tells us to go ahead and eat the cake now because that's all the reward there is (Matt 6:2). In what could have been so much more—about the kingdom—virtue is lost. It is more blessed to give than to receive, we are told (Acts 20:35); unless, of course, we give in order to receive. That's just backward in God's economy. Perhaps the best gifts are those when nothing is expected in return, not even a thank you note—acts of selfless love.

What about public prayer? "And when you pray, do not be like the hypocrites, for they love to pray standing in the synagogues and on the street corners to be seen by others" (Matt 6:5). Surely, Jesus is not telling us to avoid praying in public, is he? Well, maybe. As with giving, Jesus is concerned more about the intent of the act than the act itself. Public prayer can be so beautiful, so powerful, so formative, but when praying in public becomes more about the one who prays than the prayer, it's a problem. Jesus saw many who prayed in public, saying in effect, "Look at me, I'm so spiritual," but they didn't love God or each other. They were pretenders who loved to be in the spotlight. Prayer was a means to a personal end. Jesus' instructions were to "go into your room, close the door and pray to your Father" (Matt 6:6). That's still good advice today.

Jesus also cautioned us to avoid being too public about our religious disciplines, fasting included. "When you fast, do not look somber as the hypocrites do, for they disfigure their faces to show others they are fasting" (Matt 6:16). I think you see the pattern. Charity, prayer, and fasting are formative practices, to be sure, but they were being used for another purpose—self-seeking. We all should think twice about our motivation to pray in public, speak in church, sing on the worship team, or publically display our spirituality. Even good practices can be easily corrupted if we are not careful. This is not to say that there is no place for public religion. There certainly is, but we must be vigilant about self-seeking and honest enough to admit that it can show up in the best of us, in the best of places, too—even church.

Some Practical Advice

One of the best ways to keep from slipping into a self-seeking mode is to find ways to be a servant—to wash some feet. That is to say, purposely look for things that need to be done that are out of the limelight. You can volunteer to be an usher or greeter, or work as part of the teardown crew. After an event, most everyone goes to dinner or to a party or home, but someone has to tear down, put things away, and clean up. It's a thankless job out of the spotlight, particularly on a Saturday night when Sunday is coming. Why not step up and lend a hand? And you could help the musicians and sound techs tear down and put away equipment after the Sunday service. Help is always appreciated since they want to go home, too. You could wash dishes, help out in the nursery, weed a flower bed, vacuum a hallway, or put a classroom back in order. Just look for things that need to be done, and step in and do them. No one will stop you.

Another strategy if you struggle with self-seeking is to consciously shine the spotlight on others in conversations instead of taking center stage yourself. Start by working at not using the "I" word in conversations. Instead, ask questions and listen intently. Focus on lifting the human spirit. Everyone has a story and most will tell it to you if given half a chance. Honestly, it will be hard at first to refrain from talking about yourself but it can be done, and the dividends are huge. Try it—it won't hurt you!

Finally, give without announcement, and if you can, without public praise or recognition. This is hard work, too. It is human nature to want to be recognized, appreciated, and honored, but it can quickly transform something really good (like giving, fasting, and prayer) into something very ugly (like self-seeking, pride, and self-promotion). You can take real delight in watching the impact of your gift without anyone suspecting that you were the donor. Look this week for an opportunity to be an anonymous giver. Truly, giving faithfully and humbly is deeply rewarding. No need for fanfare.

Conclusion

Self-seeking stunts your spiritual growth and deadens the spirits of those around you, but where self-seeking ends, dignity begins. At some point, you have to let your life speak for itself, and there is genuine dignity in doing so. In this chapter, we have identified self-seeking as a bad weed, examined several modes of self-promotion—boasting, bragging, self-importance, and self-centeredness; we looked at what Jesus said about self-seeking in the Sermon on the Mount; and we offered some practical advice for dealing concretely with self-centeredness—be a servant, lift up others, and give expecting nothing in return. In doing so, we consciously take ourselves out of the limelight and lift others up. And when we do, it is Christ who is honored.

Questions for Discussion and Reflection

1. Can you think of someone who is constantly talking about himself or herself, needing to be the center of attention? How does it feel to be around them?

2. Are you more prone to boasting or bragging? That is, are you more prone to talk about what you have done, where you have traveled, or accomplished, or about things that you have or what you are currently doing? Be honest—it won't hurt you.

3. Do you know of a situation involving an anonymous gift or have you ever received one? If so, what was the result? How could you become an anonymous giver?

4. Are there activities at your church that can easily lead you to self-promotion? How can you guard against this result?

5. Do you see places of service in your church or community, ones without prestige or public rewards? Think how you can encourage and join those who work in the shadows every day.

I will try this day to live a simple, sincere, and serene life, repelling promptly every thought of discontent, anxiety, discouragement, impurity, and self-seeking . . .

* * *

The Other Road—The Rest of the Story

I began chapter 1 by telling a story about traveling the other road—how I lost the opportunity to coach the college basketball team (my dream job) because my boss took the job after telling me that it wouldn't work with his office schedule. Of course, I felt betrayed—and I was angry, too. Then, I realized that I would have to stay in the office even more to provide coverage while he was out doing what I wanted to do. I certainly wasn't going to be a happy co-worker. I had a bad attitude and I wanted to quit on the spot. In the office garden, I was a bad weed, carrying seeds of disappointment, discouragement, and an impure thought or two.

However, my best friend asked me if I had signed a contract to work through the year. I said that I had. He asked me if others were counting on me. I said that they were. He asked me if I meant it when I signed the contract or was it provisional on what others did. I said that I meant it when I signed it. He wondered if it would be the right thing to do to honor my commitments. I knew he was right, but I still didn't like it!

So, I did my job, but I brought no joy to the office. In fact, I brought a bad attitude, feeling sorry for myself. Shortly after school began, a student came in needing a signature in order to drop out of school. I said, "Okay," and signed the form without even looking up. He was almost out the door when I called to him. "Hey, just out of idle curiosity, why are you leaving school so soon?" "Oh," he said, "I don't like it here. I don't fit in. You see, I'm from Minnesota, and it is so hot here. No one knows me and no one knows anything about ice hockey." "Well, sit down," I said as I motioned to the only chair in my little office, "I'm from Michigan and I love hockey—I even have season tickets to the NHL team in town. And I don't plan on doing anything productive today, so let's have a talk." After a thirty-minute hockey conversation, I turned to Steven and said, "Look, it seems to me that you might just want to stay for the rest of this semester since you are already here. We'll talk hockey and the food in the cafeteria is really pretty good. Then, you can go home at Christmas break and not come back, and no one will be the wiser. But if you go home now, everyone will know that you quit." I guess it made some sense because he decided to stay. Before long, Steven and I were good buddies.

Near the middle of first semester, I received a call from the local authorities. They were expecting some intense local flooding and wondered if some students could come out and help. I said that I knew of one student who wasn't studying much, so I called Steven. That night, we went over to the river and helped fill sandbags. We worked alongside a group of homeless men who were promised hot coffee and warm donuts for their help. Steven seemed to appreciate the compensation, too. After a while, Steven struck up a conversation with two of the men, Bob and Tom. As we were leaving the next morning, they asked Steven if he would come visit them at the local mission sometime and stay for dinner. He said that he would.

The next Tuesday evening, Steven and I headed down to the mission and ate dinner with Bob and Tom. The dinner was preceded by a simple religious service. At dinner, Steven mentioned that he was a religion major. Immediately, Tom invited him to preach the very next week. I wasn't sure that it was even his place to make this offer, but Steven accepted the invitation on the spot. That made me really nervous, but the next Tuesday, Steven (dressed in his one and only suit and tie) and I drove back to the mission. Honestly, it was a terrible sermon, but no one seemed to notice. We helped serve dinner, ate with Bob and Tom, and drove back to campus. All in all, it was quite an evening. We became regular attendees at the mission. We called it the Tuesday Night Club.

At the end of the semester, I shook Steven's hand and said goodbye. I told him to have a good life and write when he could. I honestly thought that that would be the last of Steven, but at the start of the spring term, Steven walked into my office. He had decided to stick it out for the first year. The next Tuesday evening, we headed down to the mission to see our friends. Bob was there, but not Tom. "Oh," Bob said soberly, "Tom's not here. He's gone." "To Florida, I hope," I joked. "No," he said sadly, "he's just gone. He froze to death just down the street last week while sleeping in a cardboard box." Steven and I were stunned. Simply stunned. We couldn't speak. As we drove home, Steven finally turned to me and said, "I wonder if Tom has any family. I think they need to know." We tried for several weeks to identify any next of kin without success. A week or so later, Steven bounced into my office with an idea. He wanted to start a student ministry in our local county jail. I said that our college already had one there. "No," he insisted, "not for inmates, but for their families. You see, they can only come to visit three days a week from 11 to 1. They miss their lunch. I want to minister to them by offering a sandwich and a word of comfort." I had to admit that it was a good idea, but I told him that he would have to do all the legwork himself—I couldn't help because I was too busy in the office. He said that he would, and he did. Steven and his team were at the jail faithfully every Monday, Wednesday, and Friday for ministry. Sometimes he would bring a leftover sandwich or two back to my office, and we would have lunch together.

Later that spring semester, life hit me full in the face. Someone I dearly loved was arrested and jailed. As he awaited trial, I visited him as much as I could—every Monday, Wednesday, and Friday. It is so painful to see someone you love in such a terrible environment. Every time I visited, I left with a broken heart—but as I did, guess who ministered to me? Yes, it was Steven and his team. They offered me a sandwich of grace.

That summer, I left the college for graduate school in a neighboring state, and I lost contact with Steven. As far as I knew, he went back to Minnesota for good, having survived a year in "hot country." Ten years later, I was invited back for a wedding. I arrived a bit early and as I stood there in the vestibule of the church, a man came up to me and asked if my name was Patrick. "Yup," I grinned, "who's asking?" He smiled, too, and said, "You don't recognize me, do you?" Then it hit me. "Well, Steven, how are you? You look great! It is so good to see you. Sit with me if you can." He chuckled again, "Well, I can't. You see, I'm a minister, and I'm officiating the ceremony." He went on to tell me that for the past six years, he had been a pastor of a small church in a town with a very large state prison, and he ran a ministry for family members of inmates who lived near the prison. Imagine how I felt during that ceremony as I watched Steven pray and serve communion to the newlyweds. I thought about our time together back at college and that year of disappointment and betrayal. Do you think I really cared at that time that my boss had manipulated me out of the job as basketball coach?

Well, honestly, I still did! He lied to me and hurt me, and he shouldn't have done so, particularly while professing to be a role model. It wasn't right! I expected more than that from our leaders, and I still do. But at the same time, I must confess that the wedding was a wonderful occasion. The small part I played in Steven's ministerial preparation was deeply satisfying. I could see God's fingerprints all over the ceremony. I have come to believe in this: You can count on two things in life. First, life is messy. Either it is, has been, or will be. That's life. But you can also count on this: God is faithful. He is faithful to work in and through all things—in our victories and in our disappointments, in the good times and in the bad times. He is always faithful, and he calls us to be faithful, too.

* * *

We have examined some bad weeds in this first part of our *Morning Resolve* that can choke out our spiritual gardens. As we work to promptly repel these weeds, we know that God is with us and at work in us. We don't have to do this work alone.

— PART II —

Cultivating Healthy Attitudes and Habits

Cheerfulness, Magnanimity, Charity, and the Habit of Holy Silence

In Part I, we spent a good deal of time pulling noxious weeds. It was hard but necessary work. Now, the fun begins. In Part II, we turn our attention to cultivating some healthy attitudes and habits—cheerfulness, magnanimity, charity, and the habit of holy silence. We'll take each one in turn, developing a consistent approach to living a simple, sincere, and serene life. This is the day we start planting a garden that will flourish for a lifetime. Of course, we'll need to water and tend the new shoots, so there's still plenty of work to do. In the weeks ahead, we'll see some healthy plants look skyward!

Let's start with a story.

The Last Shot—A Story

I remember when my older brother started playing little league baseball. He was a year ahead of me in school. It was so exciting to see him in his uniform—a red hat and a blue T-shirt. It was beautiful! Oh, how I wanted to play little league, too, but alas I had to wait another year. It seems like I spent most of my childhood waiting for next year.

I would go to all the games and cheer for my brother. Then one morning the team manager called and asked if I could play that evening. Apparently, they were short one player and *very* desperate. Of course, I immediately said yes and asked for a uniform (which I wore all day). I couldn't wait for the game. This was my big break. I batted last and played right field. In the big leagues, the right fielder needs a strong arm to make the long throw from the right field corner to third base, one of the toughest throws any outfielder will be asked to make. They are some of the best athletes on the team, but not so in little league. The right fielder is the weakest fielder on the team because fewer balls are hit in that direction. All went well in the game until the third inning. A big left-handed batter came to the plate. I was petrified. What would I do if he hit the ball my way? All I could do was pray. Moments of panic can make one very spiritual. Luckily, the batter flied out to center, so I ran off the field as fast as I could and headed straight to Mom's car in the parking lot. My baseball career was over. I was ready to retire.

My mother walked over to the car and asked me what I was doing. "Nothing," I said, and started to sob. "This isn't as fun as I thought it would be, Mom. These guys are all better than me." Mom just looked at me and said, "You need to remember that just putting on a uniform doesn't make you a player. You have to practice, too. You'll get better, but since you said that you would play today, you need to get out of the car and do your best. The team needs you." I knew that she was right, of course, but I didn't like it. I made it through the game with no major fielding disasters, and I did hit the ball once—a slow roller to the second baseman. All in all, it was a wonderful day once it was over. I slept soundly that night with my ball glove tucked in its usual place under my pillow, dreaming about next year.

I want you to remember this picture of panic in right field and compare it with a second picture. Fast forward to college. When I transferred from junior college to a four-year college, I made the starting squad on the basketball team and was voted a co-captain before I ever played a game. To this day, I count that as a real honor. Our first home game against our archrival was a wild affair, the lead changing hands over a dozen times in the second half alone. When our coach called time-out with twenty seconds to go, we had the ball, but we were one point behind. In the huddle, the coach told me to take the last shot or get the ball to the other co-captain. "No problem," I said. As we walked out on the court, the co-captain came over to me and whispered, "Don't give me the ball." I looked him squarely in the eyes and said, "Don't worry, I wasn't going to." I took the shot.

Now compare these two pictures. In the first, I was afraid that I would have to field the ball; and in the second one, I wasn't going to pass up the opportunity to win the game when the ball was handed to me. What was the difference? In large part, the difference was practice—faithful practice. I practiced that last shot at least a thousand times. I would have one of my brothers count down: five, four, three, two, one—and I would take the shot. In winter, I would shovel off the driveway, cut the ends off my gloves, and practice until it was too dark to see. And in the summer after a full day of construction work, we would play five-on-five until they closed the gym. Then, I would go home and practice on our driveway until Mom would call me in the house, fearing that the neighbors might call the police.

I am convinced that there are times in life when the ball will come your way. Of course, you never know exactly what the ball will be or when it will come, but sooner or later someone or something hands the ball to you for the last shot. Whether you take the shot or pass it up will depend largely on practice, on your preparation. Let's be ready to take the shot. Let's practice.

Simply put, practice forms a person. As you seriously and faithfully embrace the disciplines and practices detailed in Part II, your spiritual life will begin to mature. There will be fruit from your labors. I invite you to join me in praying this prayer: *I will try this day to live a simple, sincere, and serene life, repelling promptly every thought of discontent, anxiety, discouragement, impurity, and self-seeking; cultivating cheerfulness, magnanimity, charity, and the habit of holy silence . . .*

Oh, by the way, that final shot—nothing but net.

— 6 —

Cheerfulness

The principles of living greatly include the capacity to face trouble with courage, disappointment with cheerfulness, and trial with humility.

—*THOMAS S. MONSON*

Introduction

I GREW UP IN a church tradition that emphasized being happy. We were all to have and share with others the "joy of the Lord." It would show the world that we were different. I remember singing, "I'm so happy and here's the reason way, Jesus took my burdens all away." Now, as a grade schooler, I'm really not sure that I carried all that many burdens, but I was glad that they were gone and sang the song with gusto nonetheless. Probably my favorite song was "I'm Happy All the Time." In fact, according to the lyrics of the song, I was not just to be happy but "in-right, outright, upright, downright happy all the time!" The song came complete with hand motions, and we sang the song through three or four times, each time a bit faster than the time before. It was fun, and in some ways, it did make me happy. To this day, I still love to sing—but not necessarily that particular song. At the same time, the not-so-subtle message I received was that Christians were to be happy—all the time. The trouble was, I wasn't, and I didn't see happiness all the time in those around me either.

Part of the problem, it seems to me, is that we confuse and confound a cheerful spirit with being happy (all the time), or funny, or even giddy. How many times have we been told to put on a happy face, even in the midst of deep pain and anguish—and especially in church? We sing praise songs, but selectively choose the texts. Everyone loves Psalm 23 ("the Lord is my shepherd, I shall not want"). So do I, but admittedly Psalm 22 hits much closer to home at times ("My God, my God, why has thou forsaken me?"). We never sing about that. Sadly, the results of such mandatory happiness are devastating, leading many to see congregational life as plastic and worship as irrelevant—and perhaps irreverent, too. That is, everyone wears a mask, our feelings, hurts, and struggles hidden. We're simply not honest with each other.

And we know that merely acting happy has a very short shelf life, too. We're not after spiritual mirth here. Going through the day with a fake smile and an insincere joviality can dry you out like an old leaf. So, can we develop the kind of cheerfulness that provides daylight for our spirits and serenity for our souls? I believe we can, but it takes practice and hard work. Cultivating isn't the most fun part of gardening, but seeing the fruits of your labors certainly is. In this chapter, we'll look at the habits and attitudes that can bring cheer to your spiritual life along with a closer examination of cheerfulness and some realistic strategies to develop and sustain it. As we have in the first five chapters of this book, we'll also consult Scripture for perspective and insight. Then, I'll end by offering some practical advice and posing some questions for discussion and reflection. Let's get to work!

Attitudes and Habits

We certainly know the opposite of cheerfulness. We see it all the time—woe, gloom, and misery—the glass is more than empty tribe. Folk with this outlook on life are just not happy, and not fun to be around either. So, why are some people so cheerful and others so gloomy? Is there a natural disposition to be one or the other? Probably. Is it a learned behavior? Partly. And if so, can you unlearn gloom? Hopefully. Maybe all that is needed is a positive mental attitude. Well, maybe. Of course, there is nothing wrong with a PMA, but I don't think you can just reason yourself into happiness any more than you can reason yourself to be a foot taller. No, it takes more than just thinking a few good thoughts—but I do know that we can work on our attitudes. Like so many things in life, I have come to believe that cheerfulness is a result of strenuous discipline. Strenuous discipline—that sounds a bit like cultivating a garden, doesn't it? Well, it is. It is work, hard work, but honest work brings contentment, and I also see a distinct connection between contentment and cheerfulness. We'll explore that connection later in this chapter.

For now, let's focus on this: cheerfulness is a habit that is formed by practice. Not a gimmick, not a quick fix, not acting happy, happy, happy all the time, but an intentional practice that over time will shape and form not only how you see the world, but how you live in it, too. We don't deny that there is darkness in the world. Of course there is, but we can choose not to live in it. So, how does one cultivate cheerfulness?

Cheer-full-ness

Optimism

To cultivate cheerfulness, being full of cheer, starts with developing an optimistic spirit. Of course, things do not always go as we would like. Circumstances can be good or bad, and usually somewhere in between. Things don't always go as we plan. That's life. In all circumstances, however, we can have a spirit of optimism. It's a choice we make. I want to be clear about this; it is a spiritual choice we make. You can't choose what happens to you, but you do choose how you react. You choose what disciplines you put into practice, and one of the most basic practices for spiritual growth is to see the good in all things, to be optimistic. And with practice, you do get better at it. For a few of us, it comes natural, but for most of us, it is a learned discipline.

Delight

Those who practice cheerfulness take a certain delight in life. It is as though they see life through a special pair of glasses. Maybe they do, but delight can be learned, too. There are two aspects to taking delight—the first is finding joy and the second is being playful. In all our lives, there are things that bring us great joy—things that fill our spirits. One of those things for me is playing guitar and singing, and another one is fishing. It is important to be intentional about such things, to know what they are, and to enjoy them often. It is a spiritual practice to do so, a way of cultivating cheerfulness. And along with finding joy, it is important to discover or rediscover our sense of play. Being around children helps, of course. They give you permission to join in. I recommend it highly. Just play with them. Be silly. Be active. It renews your spirit and brings you delight. Yes, it is delight-full.

Celebrations and Surprises

Another avenue to being full of cheer is through celebrations and surprises. Some of us don't like to be surprised, but most of us do. And even those who dislike surprises are usually in when it comes to celebrating others, their accomplishments, their promotions, and their good work. What if we made it a habit to celebrate someone and something each week? What a difference it would make in how we see the world, what we look for in each day. It is a practical and purposeful way to practice cheerfulness, to be cheerful. Just find excuses to celebrate those around you, and if you have the insight and instinct, throw in a surprise or two. It doesn't have to be much. Sharing even a coffee cake at work or with a neighbor can be a great surprise. If asked what the occasion is, just tell them that you are putting your morning resolve to cultivate cheerfulness into practice. That should start an interesting conversation.

Contentment

I believe that there is also a profound connection between cheerfulness and contentment. They are not the same thing, but they are related. One shapes the other. Those who are cheerful seem to have found a deep peace, a certain contentment with life that escapes easy explanation. They have a sense that they are in a good place, the right place. They have a sense of neighbor and community, and see themselves as a helpful part of it. In addition, contentment comes from having a sense of purpose, that what you are doing has some significance for yourself and others. In a way, there is a sense that you are on a mission, that you are here in this place at this particular time for a reason, even if the reason is not perfectly clear. Some have joked about being on a mission from God. Honestly, I think we are. Having a deep contentment that we are on a mission at this time in this place gives rise to a kind of cheerfulness that goes way beyond mirth. It is daylight for the mind and serenity for the soul.

Laughter

Not everyone is a comedian, having the gift to make people laugh. It is truly a wonderful gift. However, I am convinced that those who are cheerful have developed the ability to see humor in life, and to have a good laugh or two. They particularly have the ability to laugh at themselves. Isn't it fun to be around someone who can say to you, "You wouldn't believe what I did today," and then goes on to tell about some mistake or silly thing that happened? We laugh with them. Their joy, even in their mistakes, rubs off on each one of us. It's contagious!

Cheer-for-ness

I think I've invented this word. One of the ways to cultivate cheerfulness is to turn the focus away from our own selves and toward others. Start the practice of cheering for others. It is an outward orientation that lifts the human spirit. Find at least three things to cheer for each day. Be on the lookout—a neighbor's first volleyball match, the first or last day of school, learning to swim or drive, running a race, mowing the lawn for the first time in spring, or picking the last batch of zucchini. All of these and many more are opportunities for cheering and celebration. And in the midst of it all, you will be cheerful, too.

Scripture

In all the chapters of this book, I have tried diligently to refrain from simply quoting a verse or two from Scripture to prove my point without regard to the context of the passage; something called "proof texting." In the case of cheerfulness, I have to admit that it is tempting. The Bible does not comment often on cheerfulness. The most often quoted verses are Proverbs 15:13, "A happy heart makes the face cheerful;" Proverbs 17:22, "A cheerful heart is good medicine;" and perhaps the most often quoted verse about cheerfulness, Romans 9:7, "God loves a cheerful giver." Of course, cheerfulness does come from the heart. It is good medicine, and I'm sure that God does love a cheerful giver—so do I. However, I think there is a deeper principle to be explored. Let's look at the relationship between Saul and David.

You may remember the story of David and Goliath, the Philistine's giant warrior. David killed him with a slingshot and some smooth stones, to the great relief of the men of Israel. No one wanted to fight Goliath, who had been mocking the army of Israel for forty days and nights. When David slew Goliath and Israel won the war, a massive celebration erupted. In all the towns along the return route, women danced in the streets and sang: "Saul has slain his thousands, and David his tens of thousands" (1 Sam 18:7). At this point, we see how Saul reacted to the cheering: "Saul was very angry; this refrain displeased him greatly" (1 Sam 18:8).

As long as folk were cheering for Saul alone, he was fine. But as soon as the cheering included someone else, he didn't like it. Rather than being cheerful, he was fearful. Oh how things might have been different if Saul had joined in the cheering for David, too. David was deeply loyal to Saul. It could have been a wonderful partnership. Instead, the relationship went south and ended in tragedy. This is truly sad, but not terribly uncommon. In leadership training, we teach that it is important (even critical) to surround yourself with those who are better at key tasks than you are. The talents of others need not threaten you. In fact, you should cheer for them! Only a very sick soul insists on being the very best at everything, hiring only weak talent and pushing out those who have stronger skills. Those who do insure their organization will be mediocre at best. Remember, cheerfulness includes cheer-for-ness. Cheerful or fearful—it's a choice with interminable consequences.

Some Practical Advice

As we end this chapter, here are some practical points to employ as we seek to cultivate cheerfulness. The first step is to make practicing cheerfulness a high priority. This may almost seem silly, but it is important to remember that we are shaped by what we intentionally practice. Optimism, contentment, and delight are learned states. As we consciously focus on being cheerful, we will get better at it. Serenity is a plant to be tended. If we begin to think about the ability we have to grow what we nurture, understanding it as a gift from God rather than thinking that serenity is somehow beamed down to us while we do nothing, we'll see that there is work to be done.

The second step is to make cheerfulness a daily practice, not an occasional activity. There is no substitute for repeated effort. Earlier I wrote that God does not expect us to be perfect, but he expects us to be faithful. In this case, being faithful means keeping at it. That is one reason why we read "A Morning Resolve" each and every day. It is a reminder that there is work to be done *this* day.

One way to make cheerfulness a daily priority is to imagine that God has appointed you to be a cheerleader. As you go through each day, look for opportunities to cheer for others at work, at play, in the neighborhood, or in church. And what would it mean if you were somehow appointed to be the captain of the cheerleading squad? Who would you recruit to be part of the squad? What would you do? In San Diego, there was a group called Women of Purpose. They would get together each week and ask, "Who can we help this week?" I greatly admired their work, and I must say that they were cheerleaders, too. What if you brought a small group together each week and asked, "Who can we cheer for this week?" I bet you would have more opportunities than you could shake a stick at.

Another way to make cheerfulness a daily priority is to celebrate the small victories in life. I use the word *small* intentionally. I urge you to celebrate the small victories because major victories are so few and far between. Oh, of course, celebrate the major victories like promotions, graduations, marriages, and such, but also celebrate the small victories, too—a new bird feeder, a good week at school, learning to swim, a wonderful meal, or the first strawberries of the season. Getting into the habit of looking for small things to celebrate will bring cheerfulness to the fore. And we can celebrate forward in the same way we pay forward. Just think of times when someone has celebrated you, and how special it made you feel. Why not do the same for someone else, and tell them to pass it on? Celebrate it forward!

Finally, spend your time with cheerful people. In the long run, you become like the people you hang with, so why not seek out cheerful people? It's really that simple. Ask them why they are so cheerful, where the contentment and optimism come from. Most will take it as a real compliment that you are interested enough to ask and will give you a thoughtful answer. When they do, listen and learn from them. Learning to get the word "I" out of conversations and asking questions is an honest spiritual practice. If you ask the right questions, you can learn more than you can imagine.

Conclusion

In this chapter, we have focused on how to cultivate cheerfulness. It isn't the same thing as being happy all the time, but joy, contentment, and optimism do play an important part in your spiritual growth. It is important to understand that cheerfulness can be intentionally practiced, that cultivating cheerfulness *is* a spiritual practice, and that the fruits of this labor are deeply rewarding. Cheerfulness is a wonderfully fragrant plant in any spiritual garden. It makes the other plants more enjoyable, too. It never crowds them out.

Questions for Discussion and Reflection

1. When you really need to restore your spirit, what do you do? What kinds of activities bring you the most joy?

2. Who do you know that is the most fun to be around? What makes them so? What can you learn from them and put into practice?

3. What aspect of contentment is most difficult for you right now—having a sense of right place, a sense of right purpose, or a sense of right timing? What might you do about it?

4. Think about the last time someone celebrated something in your life. How did it make you feel? Could you return the favor or "celebrate forward?" How?

5. Your assignment is to be a cheerleader for someone this week. Can you think of a way to do this that is unexpected—even fun? And who could you recruit for your cheerleading squad?

I will try this day to live a simple, sincere, and serene life, repelling promptly every thought of discontent, anxiety, discouragement, impurity, and self-seeking; cultivating cheerfulness . . .

Magnanimity

Knowledge alone is not enough. It must be leavened with magnanimity before it becomes wisdom.

−ADLAI EWING STEVENSON

Introduction

I HAVE TROUBLE EVEN pronouncing *magnanimity*, let alone trying to explain what it means and how to pursue it. According to most definitions, magnanimity—derived from the Latin roots *magna* (great) and *animus* (mind or spirit)—is the virtue of being great of mind and heart. It encompasses a refusal to be petty or vindictive, a willingness to face life with dignity and courage, and an inclination toward gracious and generous actions, either literally or in spirit. No wonder Aristotle called it the crowning virtue. It is certainly the kind of spiritual plant that we want to flourish in our gardens.

However, with all due respect to Aristotle, when I think of magnanimity, I think of Mrs. Regan, my fourth-grade teacher. She was certainly one of the most influential persons in my early life, but our relationship got off on the wrong foot. For some reason, we just didn't click during that year. In fact, when I left the classroom on the final day of the school year, I said to Mrs. Regan, "I don't like school very much, I don't like you very much, and I'm glad that you won't be my teacher next year." Even as I write this, I am embarrassed. Honestly, I think I was a pretty good kid, so this seems quite out of character. Nonetheless, there it is; I said it.

All went well until I returned for school the following fall. Mrs. Regan had been assigned a fifth-grade classroom, and guess who was in her room. Yikes! As I came to the classroom door, there stood Mrs. Regan, smiling. She leaned down and said to me in a whisper, "Do you remember what you said to me as you left the classroom last spring?" I said, "No," even though I remembered every painful word—words that I now wanted so very much to somehow take back. She looked at me with unexpected kindness and undeserved compassion and said, "I don't remember either. Let's make this a good year. In fact, I was wondering if you would consider serving as my science lab assistant this year?" It was an act of grace. I accepted on the spot!

It was during that fifth-grade year that learning came alive for me. As Mrs. Regan's science lab assistant, I arranged the chairs in straight rows, washed the blackboards, and put away the lab equipment (such as there was). For me, however, it was much more than just being a helper. She would talk to me about learning, and how proud she was of my work and my new attitude. She said that she just knew that I could be a good student if I wanted to, and I became one. She saw more in me than I thought was there.

Years later, Mrs. Regan told my mother that she was deeply disturbed by my parting comments as I left her fourth-grade classroom, and she wanted a do-over. She requested a fifth-grade assignment and specifically asked that I be assigned to her room. She thought all summer about how to get me hooked on learning because she saw so much potential in me. Her idea was to have me serve as the science lab assistant so she would have a few moments each day to talk to me about school and offer some encouragement. That was all it took. To this day, I love learning and I get excited about the first day of school, even though I now work with doctoral students. I seriously doubt that you would be reading this book right now if it had not been for Mrs. Regan and the magnanimity she extended to me. She was "great of mind and heart." She refused to be vindictive even though she had every reason and resource to do so. Rather, she was generous and kind beyond belief, and I have tried to live my life in that way ever since.

Being Great of Mind and Heart

So, how do we cultivate magnanimity in our own lives? Clearly, some folk are better at it than others. Is it just innate, some have it and some don't? Are we born that way? Well, not exactly. While I admit that it comes more naturally for some than for others, I do believe that all of us can get better at it. That is, we can and will be shaped by what we intentionally practice. Magnanimity can be cultivated.

To use the spiritual garden metaphor, clearly magnanimity is a delicate plant. It is easily choked out by negativity, the things we worked on in Part I. And it takes a rich soil to flourish, full of nutrients. Our own character feeds it. In other words, treating others with respect and dignity flows from our own sense of dignity—a dignity of soul. If we lack self-respect, self-confidence, and self-worth, it is unlikely that we will be able to extend magnanimity in large measure to others. As is often the case, who we are and how we see ourselves influence what we are able to do. Being great of mind and heart requires a certain dignity of soul. That is, you can't extend to others that which you do not have. The first step in the practice of magnanimity is to be sure that you love yourself in a way that your neighbor would want to be loved, too. Dignity of soul is the rich soil in which magnanimity will flourish, and we will have more to say about this in the section providing practical advice.

What does the practice of magnanimity look like? I see three interrelated facets to being great of mind and heart: a redemptive response, a sustaining kindness, and an affirming vision.

Redemptive Response

After noting that he had witnessed a good deal of "mess" in his line of work over the years, I asked a senior denominational church leader what advice he would give to up-and-coming leaders in all walks of life. Without hesitation, he said, "Choose the redemptive solution when you can." That's magnanimity in action. You see it in Mrs. Regan's response to an embarrassed fifth grader. She had all the power and every right to call me to task and ask for an apology. She could have embarrassed me, too. Instead, she extended grace—a redemptive response aimed at the restoration of a relationship, not at retribution. Any time someone has the power and opportunity to be vindictive and petty, but chooses to be generous, kind, and forgiving, magnanimity is being practiced. And when someone is kind and forgiving when they have every right to be otherwise, the spirit of Christ is at work, too.

Sustaining Kindness

Sometimes kindness isn't all that kind. Have you ever had someone flatter you with words or do something for you, but rather than being kind, you get the feeling that they are really trying to get some information from you or pander to you in some way? That brand of kindness is shallow and insincere, leaving you feeling empty—and wanting to take a quick shower, too. Sustaining kindness is different. It is genuine, heartfelt, and honest. It lifts your spirit and leaves you with your dignity intact. The key to sustaining kindness is that the dignity of the person is as important as the act itself. And when kindness is extended with the intention of an ongoing relationship, it signals something even more. It signals that you are there for the long haul. Such kindness is truly spiritual, sustaining both mind and heart.

Affirming Vision

Mrs. Regan not only made sure that the unkind way I left fourth grade was rectified (a redemptive response with sustaining kindness), she also saw more in me than I saw in myself. She thought that I could become a good student, and she was determined to make it happen for me. Most of us have had persons in our lives who saw more in us than our talents would indicate, and believed in us more than was sensible. In essence, they saw into the future; it was grace with a forward lean. The power of an affirming vision is almost beyond description. Those who practice magnanimity see the best in others, and speak into their lives in positive and hopeful ways. It costs nothing, but it means everything.

Before we explore some practical ways to cultivate magnanimity in our own lives and conclude with some questions for discussion and reflection, let's look at a story from Scripture that gives us great insight into how Jesus practiced magnanimity. It is no wonder that Jesus was called the Teacher, and he continues to teach us even today.

Scripture

You may be familiar with the story of Simon and his brother, Andrew. They were the first two Jesus called to be his disciples. Since they were both commercial fishermen, it was a surprising choice. They didn't have any obvious skills to serve in such a high-profile capacity. Apparently, Jesus saw more in them than anyone else. In fact, he had an affirming vision for them both, and particularly so for Simon. When Simon confessed that Jesus was the Messiah (recorded in Matt 16, Mark 8, Luke 9), Jesus gave him a new name—Peter (the rock)—and a new mission ("upon this rock I will build my church").

However, Peter, the rock, turned out to be a bit of a rolling stone. He talked a big game, but when it came right down to it, he denied knowing Christ three times in a single night—just as Jesus had predicted he would (Matt 26, Mark 14, Luke 22, John 18). He must have felt terrible, and a bit embarrassed, too. After Jesus' death, what were he and his friends to do, particularly given their very public failure to stand with Jesus? They did what they knew to do; they went fishing. Imagine how Peter and company must have felt when after going back to their old work, Jesus came, gave them a marvelous catch, and then cooked breakfast. With sustaining kindness, Jesus talked to Peter and gave him a new charge: "Feed my sheep" (John 21:17). It was a redemptive response of the highest level. Jesus not only reconciled with Peter, but also reaffirmed his mission in terms that he could understand. I doubt if Peter had any idea about how to build a church, but he could certainly care for the flock—and he did. God doesn't expect us to know and plan out everything in advance. Instead, he calls us to be faithful. Peter did what he knew to do, and God honored his call. He will honor ours, too, in magnanimous ways.

Some Practical Advice

Thus far in this chapter, we've defined magnanimity, examined the three primary aspects entailed in the practice of this virtue (a redemptive response, a sustaining kindness, and an affirming vision), observed the magnanimity of Jesus in his relationship with Simon Peter, and acknowledged that there is a lesson there for each of us. What follows are five practical ways to put magnanimity into practice.

First, start by taking a careful assessment of yourself, your own self-esteem and self-confidence. As we noted earlier, we are instructed to love our neighbors as ourselves. This, of course, implies that we love ourselves in a manner that our neighbors would want to be loved. So, start by taking stock. Do you struggle with issues of self-worth? If so, talk to someone—a trusted friend, a spiritual director, or a professional. Don't try this alone. Before you attempt to intentionally practice being magnanimous, first be magnanimous with yourself. I think a good place to start is with the affirmation that you are God's beloved. He has called you and loves you deeply. That will never change.

Second, admit that being kind and gracious are not always your first inclinations. There are those in our lives who have been unkind and hurtful to us. When the shoe is on the other foot, it is so tempting to give them some of their own medicine. I know, I've been there, too, but we don't have to act on our very first inclination. Instead, we can choose the redemptive solution. It's our choice, you know. Returning good for evil is not always easy, but it is the right thing to do whether it is ever acknowledged or not. We ultimately live by the choices we make and the things we practice. We can be intentional about choosing the redemptive solution when there is one.

Third, in situations where grace and forgiveness are extended, take the next step and think about how an ongoing relationship could be established, maintained, or restored. Practicing magnanimity is more than reconciliation, as important as this first step is. Moving from reconciliation to relationship is really the goal. Jesus could have just forgiven Peter, but he did much more to reaffirm their relationship and his calling. Jesus didn't let Peter's failings, as real as they were, stand in the way of a relationship with him. This is a good example for all of us from the wisest teacher I know.

Fourth, you can practice speaking into the future. We all know of those who have great potential and talent, but they don't see it in themselves. Often, they are family members or very close friends. It is grace at work to speak into their lives, telling what you see in them and what possibilities you see for them. When you do this, in essence you are giving them a new name. Of course, it may not be a literal new name, but it is literally a new identity—a new way for them to think of themselves. This is certainly a magnanimous gift, a blessing of the highest order.

Finally, as long as we are thinking about giving someone close to us a new name, why not give yourself a new one, too? Is it possible that we downplay our own abilities, talents, and potential? I think so. I'm not speaking of bragging or arrogance here, but rather I am asking all of us to humbly acknowledge that we have been given much, and challenging each of us to see ourselves as God sees us. If we are called to love others as we love ourselves, then loving ourselves is the starting place. Maybe a new name is in order.

Conclusion

In this chapter, we've acknowledged that magnanimity is a tender plant, needing tender care and nurture, but a powerful practice—a crowning virtue, according to Aristotle. Three interrelated aspects of magnanimity were discussed: a redemptive response, a sustaining kindness, and an affirming vision. Then, after seeing how Jesus practiced magnanimity with Simon Peter, five practical words of advice were offered: carefully assess your own life first; choose the redemptive solution even when your inclination is to do otherwise; after reconciliation, focus on relationship; give someone a new name; and give yourself a new name, too.

At the end of the day, we have to admit that cultivating magnanimity is not for the faint of heart. As with the cultivation of so many helpful and hopeful attitudes and habits, it is hard and persistent work. But it is honest work, and kingdom work, too.

Questions for Discussion and Reflection

1. In our culture, which of these three is the biggest challenge: self-respect, self-confidence, or self-worth? Why it this so? Are any of these a struggle for you?

2. Think of a time when someone extended undeserved or unexpected grace to you? How did it make you feel? What do you think is the biggest obstacle in extending forgiveness to others in our culture? For you?

3. Think of a time when you not only extended forgiveness to someone, but also worked hard to maintain an ongoing relationship. What were the major impediments, and what made it successful? Are there any unresolved relationships in your life that need to be addressed?

4. Can you think of someone who "gave you a new name?" That is, they spoke into your life and saw more in you than you saw in yourself. How did you respond to that affirmative vision? Is there someone in your life who needs a new name?

5. If you were going to give yourself a new name, what would it be? How can you boldly step into the future?

I will try this day to live a simple, sincere, and serene life, repelling promptly every thought of discontent, anxiety, discouragement, impurity, and self-seeking; cultivating cheerfulness, magnanimity . . .

— 8 —

Charity

*The simplest acts of kindness are by far more powerful than
a thousand heads bowing in prayer.*

—MAHATMA GANDHI

Introduction

WHEN WE THINK OF charity, we usually think of giving money to someone
in need or to an organization that helps those in need. Of course, this is
needed and noble to do. Since we will focus specifically on both the positive
and negative aspects of giving money in chapter 10, I will not talk much
about that here. Instead, we will explore other facets of giving, ways to be
generous with what we have—even if you have very little by the standards
of this world. God's economy is quite different. Generosity, it turns out, has
more to do with your heart than your wallet.

In this chapter, I want to talk about charity that demands more from
you than a check and a pat on the head. I am thinking here about costly
charity—not mail-in charity, cheap charity. In our society, we are so inclined to do things at a distance. We send an email rather than sit down
for a meal. We shop online rather than visit a local store. We take online
courses from a nearby university. We use Skype with our neighbors. We
fight our wars from 30,000 feet. We even send a text message to family
members who are in the same house! In so many ways, we live disconnected lives. Sadly, our front porches are largely a thing of the past. Now, I am

not trying to disregard the benefits of technology in our society (for there are many), but I am concerned that we pay a price for it, too. In too many ways and on too many occasions, the convenience provided by technology comes at the cost of authentic relationships and personal connections, and that can result in a kind of desperate isolation and alienation. This, it seems to me, is not healthy.

So, what does costly charity, charity that demands something from you, look like? I have come to believe that charity has more to do with loving than it has to do with giving. At least, that's is a good place to start. Let's examine three ways to put love into charity; what I call "giving with heart."

The first way to put love into charity is to *show up, to be fully present*. That is, donate your time, use your talents, focus your attention, and offer personal affirmation and encouragement whenever possible. Why is this so much more powerful than just sending a check? For starters, time is very valuable. Some say that time *is* money. In our busy world, time may be more valuable than money since there are only so many hours in a day. When you give of your time, you are making a statement that that activity or person is worth a great deal to you. So important, in fact, that you are willing to invest your time and energies for them and in them.

In addition, when you give of your time, you have the opportunity to use your talents, to give personal attention to others, and to be a voice of encouragement. All these acts build relationships and partnerships. It is love in action. Think of the difference between a neighbor giving you fifty dollars to help pay for your new driveway and rolling up his or her sleeves, helping you pour concrete on a Saturday morning. With the former, you save fifty dollars, but with the latter, relationships and bonds of friendship are strengthened. That, it seems to me, is worth far more than fifty dollars. It is giving with heart.

The second way to practice charity with love is to *give the benefit of the doubt*. Of course, this is not easy to do. Some say it is not wise either; people will take advantage of you. Honestly, some will. And others say it is not responsible; it isn't the way the world works. To get ahead, you don't trust anyone. You always expect the worst from folk and prepare for it, and that includes your co-workers, friends, and relatives. To always give the benefit of the doubt is just plain foolish. Maybe so, but there will be times when giving the benefit of the doubt is a good thing. After all, your doubts can be wrong. And isn't that how you would like to be treated at home, at work, at church, and around your community? Doesn't the Golden Rule come into play here? Giving grace is an act of charity with love, and if some take advantage of you for extending grace, so what? Are you diminished by the choices others make? Perhaps the best way to cultivate charity in our lives is simply to resolve to see the best in others, to give the benefit of the doubt. It's not cheap charity.

A third way to cultivate charity in your life is perhaps the most difficult: to *give in for the sake of the relationship*. It is one thing to give the benefit of the doubt when you are uncertain of the details, but what about when you know that you are right? What about when someone is clearly in the wrong, and you are the one who has been snubbed or treated shabbily? What about then? Don't you have every right to be frustrated and angry? Are you expected to be charitable then, too? The simple answer to this very complex set of questions goes something like this: you don't have to be charitable, but in many cases, you can be. It's a choice you make. Clearly, there are times when you need to sever a relationship that is unhealthy and hurtful. When these situations arise, obviously you need to do whatever is necessary to prevent further injury, pain, and suffering. Personal boundary maintenance is crucial. However, it is also important to remember that we are all "cracked pots." We have all come up short on more than one occasion, and we aren't always at our best. And since we serve a God who wouldn't let our failings and sin stand in the way of the possibility of a relationship with him, can we make every effort to do the same with others? Surely, it is costly charity, but giving in for the sake of the relationship, even when we have every right to do otherwise, is a spiritual practice that not only cultivates charity in our own lives, but also has the potential to undergird and sustain relationships that would otherwise end.

Thus far, we have examined practicing charity with love in three dimensions: giving of yourself, giving the benefit of the doubt, and giving in for the sake of the relationship. To be sure, these are all costly forms of charity, and they require consistent cultivation to take root. Before extending some practical advice for practicing charity, we will look to Scripture for insight.

Scripture

In Genesis (37–50), the first book of the Old Testament, we find the wonderful story about Joseph and his coat of many colors. It is certainly a fascinating story full of intrigue, betrayal, good fortune, and grace upon grace. You will recall that Joseph was his father's favorite, and this didn't sit well with his brothers. It could be that Joseph flaunted this relationship and his fine outerwear a bit too much. In any case, his brothers first decided to kill him, but instead sold him to some slave traders who were passing by. Through a series of incredible events, Joseph became one of the most powerful men in Egypt, in charge of all grain distribution during a great drought that would last seven years. What happened next is almost too much to believe. Joseph's brothers, the same clan that sold him into slavery, showed up in hopes of buying some grain for their families back home. They didn't recognize him, but he surely recognized them. This was his chance to balance the scales. So, what did Joseph do? What would you have done?

It seems to me that Joseph had four courses of action open to him. First, he had every right to punish his brothers for their past crimes, and he had the power to do so. What they did was mean-spirited and criminal, deliberate actions that brought pain and suffering not only to him but to his father as well. Joseph was now an important and powerful man. With one command, he could have had his brothers arrested, tortured, and even killed. No one would have questioned him about it. After all, he was an innocent victim and they had it coming. True, he was and they did, but it is not the course of action that Joseph chose.

Second, Joseph could have sent them away without food. As his brothers were facedown on the floor begging for grain, Joseph could have spoke out, "Are you kidding me? You sell me to slave traders, tearing me away from my family and all that I loved, and now you want me to sell you food? You can't be serious. Go away. You're lucky that I don't have you arrested right here on the spot!" He would have been justified in doing so, and sending them away without food after a good tongue-lashing would have been better than they deserved. It was certainly much better than taking an eye for an eye. He had every right to do that, but that isn't what Joseph did.

A third course of action for Joseph would have been to show extreme charity by selling his brothers some food and sending them on their way home, even if they had to pay a premium for the grain. They came for food. He could give them some even though they didn't deserve it. It would have been cheap charity, but charity nonetheless. He didn't do that either.

Joseph chose a fourth course of action. He not only sold them food, but he gave then back their money, too. Wow, now that's charity with grace! Truly, it was, but there was more—much more. Joseph not only sold them food and gave their money back, but he also worked to restore their fractured relationships—the very same relationships that his brothers destroyed in the first place. And to top it off, he sent wagons so that his brothers and their families (and his father) could move to Egypt and live in plenty during the remaining five years of famine. I cannot think of a better example of giving in for the sake of the relationship. It was totally undeserved, to be sure, but the end result was nothing short of remarkable. I think what Joseph did, this lavishing of grace upon grace, is also an example of what God has done and is doing for each of us. The cultivation of charity in our spiritual gardens is so vital in large part because we have all been given so much.

Some Practical Advice

Before we end this chapter, I want to offer several words of practical advice for cultivating charity in your life. The first is to remember that you don't have to try to change the world with your charity. That's not your job. Rather, you are called to be a faithful presence where you are located. Sometimes the idea of acting with charity becomes overwhelming, particularly so if you feel that there must be enormous results with lots of accolades and public notoriety. Honestly, that's not the way most charitable activities work. In fact, when being charitable becomes more about being noticed than about helping others and restoring relationships, it is like salt that has lost its flavor. It doesn't do much for anyone.

Perhaps the biggest challenge to cultivating charity is finding the time in your busy schedule to get involved somewhere or with someone. To be fair, it does take time. I suggest that you map out your schedule a week or month at a time. Take a close look at where you spend your time. Perhaps something could be eliminated, even though they are all worthwhile activities. It often helps to audit your schedule with someone who knows you very well, perhaps a mentor or spiritual director. Sometimes it is difficult to see how things could be different without the insight of others. Also, look for a time or two when you could get involved. Make an appointment with yourself just as you would if you were going to see the dentist. I find that if I make appointments, I keep them. If I don't, the time gets filled with all sorts of other activities.

It is also helpful to do an analysis of your own skills and abilities. What do you do well? What do you like to do? Then, find an organization or activity that could use some help with the skills you have. For example, I have a graduate degree in management, and I love to do strategic planning. While it is certainly okay for me to help with trimming the trees around town, it seems much more productive if I can find an organization or two that needs help with their planning. Perhaps these organizations will grow and flourish, and the trees, left to those who know what they are doing, will have a better chance to grow and flourish, too.

One final thought before we conclude this chapter, and I want to be careful to communicate this accurately. We talked about costly charity, charity that seeks to reestablish fractured relationships. It is the kind of charity that Joseph practiced. This is, it seems to me, kingdom work. Perhaps you can think of a relationship that has seen better days. If so, is it possible to find a tangible way to offer an olive branch, to give it another chance? Could you invite that person to meet you for a coffee or to watch a little league game? You can't control how that person might respond to such a gesture, but that's totally up to her or him, isn't it? You might just give it a try if you feel so inclined.

However, before you head into any such endeavor, please talk it over with a trusted friend or advisor. There can be damaging, hurtful, and toxic relationships that you have no business trying to restore, even though at times you may feel guilt or shame about them. Cultivating charity does not mean that you are to put your well-being in harm's way, and honestly, if you have been hurt, it is sometimes very difficult to see realistically the prospects for restoration. Some relationships just lead to additional pain. It is a spiritual practice to care for your well-being, too. We'll have much more to say about this in Part IV. Suffice it here to say that cultivating costly charity takes discernment, a practice that is better done with others. We really do need each other.

Conclusion

There are many dimensions to the spiritual practice of charity. In this chapter, we considered three: being present, giving the benefit of the doubt, and giving in for the sake of the relationship. We then looked at the story of Joseph from Genesis, and saw that although he had every right to be vindictive, he practiced costly charity. Not only did he give his brothers what they needed (food), he also worked diligently and purposely to restore a lifetime of broken relationships. In doing so, he foreshadowed the work that God wants to do in each of our lives, too. We then offered four words of practical advice: don't think that you have to change the world, do a calendar audit, focus on your own skills and abilities, and work to restore relationships—but do so carefully, prayerfully, and corporately.

I would like to conclude with these two questions. First, what if you thought of wealth as the accumulation of what good you do in the world instead of what things you can accumulate from the world? This is such an important distinction, isn't it? Far too often, we think of wealth in terms of the stuff we have. Not so in God's economy. And second, since "you really can't take it with you," isn't it what you give and the impact you have on others that will live beyond you in a meaningful way? This is another reason why I believe the cultivation of charity is so vitally important in our spiritual lives. It is a practice with eternal implications.

Questions for Discussion and Reflection

1. Have you recently audited your calendar? Do you think you could find several times each month to practice charity? If you made an appointment with yourself each week, what would be the biggest impediment to keeping it faithfully?

2. List out your three best talents, skills, or abilities. Can you think of an organization that could use them? If not, can you ask someone for guidance?

3. Can you think of any of your current charitable activities (giving to Goodwill, mission trips, school or church activities) where you might also work to be in relationship, too? How could you go about doing that?

4. How are you at giving the benefit of the doubt? Is this an easy practice for you, or do you think it is ripe for disappointment and hurt? If the latter, what could you do to make it less so?

5. As you read this chapter, did a relationship come to mind that needs restoration? How could you go about cultivating charity in this case?

I will try this day to live a simple, sincere, and serene life, repelling promptly every thought of discontent, anxiety, discouragement, impurity, and self-seeking; cultivating cheerfulness, magnanimity, charity . . .

— 9 —

The Habit of Holy Silence

*God is the friend of silence . . . . We need silence to be able
to touch souls.*

—*MOTHER TERESA*

Introduction

THE FIRST TIME I read "A Morning Resolve," I was captivated by the idea
of cultivating the habit of holy silence. What a wonderful spiritual discipline, one most of us could get better at. In this chapter, we will explore the
meaning of holy silence and examine ways to see it grow and prosper in
our spiritual gardens. First, however, let me start with two confessions. The
first one is this: silence is not an easy thing to practice, particularly so in a
culture that focuses so much on entertainment, music, television, personal
messages, conversations, advertisements, and so much more. We are deeply
enmeshed in a noisy culture—noise on steroids, if you will, and nourished
by technology. Honestly, many of us cannot even take a short walk without
listening to music or checking our phones for messages. In many ways, we
have grown wildly unfamiliar with silence, and it makes us uncomfortable,
too. It is hard to think about cultivating the habit of holy silence when the
very idea of silence is foreign and somehow frightening to so many of us.

I must also confess that not all silence is holy. There is an unholy silence, the kind of silence that buries the truth or turns a blind eye to those
in their hour of need. You experience it when you lose or leave your job or

church. You suddenly become invisible. A lot of folk will talk about you, but very few will talk to you. The silence can be deafening. There is also a kind of bullied silence that is enforced by power and fed by fear. There is a kind of silence that hides the truth and protects persons and organizations that do wrong. It is a shameful silence desperately trying to protect an image and cover up sin. And far too often, there is a silence that stems from our unwillingness to stand up and speak out against injustice and meanness—even in our own neighborhoods. We drive by and watch the house burn, but we don't stop and try to help put out the fire. No one wants to get involved.

I readily admit that it is easy to be critical of such behaviors from a distance. I get that. But I also know that when truth is replaced by silence, we are all diminished in significant ways—whether the silence is practiced in our homes, our neighborhoods, our churches, our corporations, or our governments. Sadly, unholy silence is nurtured when courage, conviction, and compassion wane.

Of course, there are more familiar forms of unholy silence, too, forms that take root in the events of our daily lives. There is the silence that communicates disapproval. It is often a multigenerational family practice. It goes something like this: "If you do something I don't like or you don't do something I want you to do, then I won't speak to you." It is silence used as punishment. This lesson can be learned at a very early age, and the sins of the father and mother are often visited upon the next generation or two. Honestly, most of us can point to relatives and friends who are not speaking to each other, and sadly, most of us engage in this behavior more than we care to admit. Rarely is withholding communication or totally ignoring someone a holy practice.

(A quick caveat is in order here. I am not saying that you need to be best buddies with everyone, and certainly not with those who have hurt you or treated you with malice and disrespect. I am not even arguing here for frequent communication. There is no need for a phone call every Sunday evening. However, I am saying that to remain civil, in most instances, is a healthy practice, and possibly the best way to keep the door of reconciliation open—even if just a crack.)

Silence can also be used to marginalize others. Have you ever entered a room and the conversation suddenly stops? Do you remember how awkward that made you feel? Did you somehow intrude into a private conversation, or was the conversation about you or someone close to you? Most likely you will never know, but the silence made it clear that you were not welcome in that conversation. Silence that intentionally marginalizes is simply hurtful and wrong. It is not a holy practice.

Surely, there must be a more healthy approach to the practice of silence. Can it ever be a good thing, a holy thing? Fortunately, the answer is yes. The good news is that the habit of holy silence can be cultivated. It takes practice, of course, but as you will see, it is well worth the effort.

Holy Silence

I want to focus on three constructive practices as we work to cultivate the habit of holy silence: keeping quiet, being present, and listening. These activities are not earthshaking, but they are formative. That is to say, if they are undertaken with intention, they will shape you.

Keeping Quiet

I am not very good at being quiet, let alone keeping quiet. My father, sounding a bit like Will Rogers, would offer this advice: "Never miss a good opportunity to keep quiet." He was right, of course. So, what does it mean to practice keeping quiet? First, you don't have to repeat everything you hear. Why is it so compelling to pass on a bit of juicy gossip about someone? We even promise not to pass it along in order to hear the gossip in the first place, and then turn right around and pass it on, too—but only after making the next person promise that they won't pass it on either! We've all done it. What if we made a firm commitment to only pass on good things? It would take sincere effort, but I think we could do it, and we would be better for it.

A related aspect of keeping quiet is to keep negative thoughts and criticisms a private matter. I don't know of a single spiritual director who would advocate that it is a healthy practice to tell everything that comes to mind. Keeping quiet means more than just not telling what you hear, it's also not telling all that you think—especially if it is critical. Criticism is hard enough to take when you ask for it. Uninvited criticism (even if it is intended to be constructive) is about as welcome as a swarm of bees at a picnic. And speaking of unwelcome, it is best to avoid the "I told you so" line—even if you did. At the time, it just isn't helpful to mention to someone who fell into the water that you did say it would be better to stand clear of the riverbank. It is *so* tempting, but keeping quiet is a much better practice.

Perhaps the most difficult aspect of keeping quiet is not responding in kind. For example, refraining from yelling back when someone is yelling at you, or from talking poorly about the one who is spreading rumors about you. It is so challenging to keep quiet in such circumstances. Practicing holy silence will not always be comfortable or easy, but it starts by attempting to keep quiet when encountering gossip, criticism, or uncivil behavior.

Being Present

There are times when words are unnecessary, and times when there are no fitting words at all. When sitting with someone who has just lost a career or a loved one, or with someone who has just been told that the illness is terminal, there are really no words to express the depth of pain, discouragement, shock, and fear that one is feeling—and you certainly cannot simply talk them away. At such times, you express all you need to say by just being present. A simple hug or a touch of the hand can say a million words. In such situations, I believe our spirits do commune. No words are necessary.

Being present also means to faithfully walk alongside someone who is facing a deep crisis or a genuine adventure. True friends let you know that they are with you for the long haul, and then practice the habit of holy silence. When parents watch their kids drive off, they smile and wave goodbye from the front porch. Many times they are also praying a silent, desperate prayer. In outright success and in downright failure, their children know that they can count on their parents—not to second-guess them, but to always be present when needed. The door is always open. Such presence is, indeed, holy.

Listening

Listening intentionally and carefully is a gift, and listening without giving answers and advice is an act of holy silence. I've found that instead of saying, "You know what you should do" or "If I were you, I would . . . ," it is far more helpful to simply say, "My, My," and nod my head. It is the most supportive thing I know to say. In most cases, there is more comfort extended in silence than in the answer to a question, no matter how directly the question is put. Of course, this is a learned behavior. My native response is to give unsolicited advice or to wax eloquent. But truthfully, such advice is seldom fruitful.

The art of listening that leads to holy silence often starts with an insightful or caring question. The key is to refrain from talking about or interjecting your favorite subject into the conversation—you. Avoid the words, *I, me,* and *my,* if you possibly can. This is a terribly hard thing to do, of course, but honestly no one is as interested in your opinions and ideas as you think, not even your mother. Practicing holy silence means carefully asking good questions and then letting others speak.

And we can practice the habit of holy silence when we pray, too. In so many of our prayers, we talk to God. This is certainly good since we have much to talk to God about, sharing our cares, our dreams, our disappointments, and our hurts. God is certainly a good listener. Most of us, however, spend a good deal less time listening to God. We pray as if God is waiting to hear from us but has nothing to say to us. Of course, there is a long Christian tradition of meditation, waiting in silence to hear from God, but honestly, most of us do not practice this much. It is hard to do. Cultivating the habit of holy silence requires us to listen more and to speak less. This is countercultural.

Scripture

Let's look at two activities highlighted in Scripture that are intimately associated with the habit of holy silence—*waiting and watching.* They can be spiritual disciplines, too.

Waiting

Waiting is not an easy discipline—waiting for the phone to ring, waiting for a job interview, waiting for a package to arrive, waiting for a child to come home, waiting for the results of a biopsy. Honestly, I find it hard to wait patiently, but at some time or other, we must all do it. It is a discipline that can be a tangible expression of hope, and we find this connection between waiting and hoping in Scripture. "I remain confident of this: I will see the goodness of the Lord in the land of the living" (Ps 27:13). This is certainly an expression of hope for the future, seeing the goodness of the Lord in this land, not just in the next. And in the very next verse, "Wait for the Lord: be strong and take heart and wait for the Lord" (Ps 27:14). We hope for what is to come, and we wait.

Waiting is also connected to hope in God's word: "I wait for the Lord, my whole being waits, and in his word I put my hope" (Ps 130:5), and hope in the appearance of Jesus, "we wait for the blessed hope" (Titus 2:13). Paul, who is not one to mince words, makes the most direct connection, "Who hopes for what they already have? But if we hope for what we do not have, we wait for it patiently" (Rom 8:24–25). But how can we wait patiently? We can and do because "we know that in all things God works for the good . . ." (Rom 8:28). We wait patiently, hopefully, because we know and rely on the character of God. Wherever we are and whatever we face, we know that God loves us deeply and is there in the mess with us, working to redeem even the worst of situations. So, we wait and hope, and we wait with hope. We wait in holy silence.

Watching

Waiting and watching are closely related. We wait at the kitchen window, watching the driveway for the first glimpse of our grandparent's car. We watch the clock, waiting for the cake to bake or the workweek to be over. And we watch the calendar, waiting for a birthday or the 25th of December. In a culture of activity and instant gratification, watching and waiting are, at best, inconveniences. In Scripture, watching or keeping watch has several meanings. In Genesis, for example, Laban says to Jacob, "May the Lord keep watch between you and me when we are away from each other" (Gen 31:49). Now, this is a father-in-law telling his son-in-law that he had better take good care of his daughters. And if he doesn't, he will be in trouble because God is watching. In this case, keeping watch means *keeping score*. Even though Laban brings God into the equation, I do not see God as the great scorekeeper in the sky, just watching for our failures. Honestly, these are not the actions of a loving God. When we, any of us, keep score for the purpose of retribution, retaliation, or simply to get ahead, we are not cultivating the habit of holy silence.

Fortunately, Scripture also portrays watching in more positive ways. One way that watching is used in Scripture means *to keep watch*. That is, to be vigilant—alert, attentive, ready. We are told to keep watch because we do not know the day and hour of the Lord's return (Matt 24:42, Luke 2:8). And you may recall that Jesus asked several of his disciples to watch and pray with him in the garden of Gethsemane, and he lost patience with them when they could not stay awake (Matt 26: 40). Obviously, keeping watch requires that we be present and awake, observant to what is happening around us. I think this includes watching for new possibilities, too. What if we would earnestly pray and ask God to show us new ways to help the kingdom come—and then keep watch? I can only imagine what we might see.

Watching over is another way to think about watching, referring to the way that shepherds watch over their flocks, providing care and protection. It is no coincidence that shepherds play such a significant role in the Advent story (Luke 2:8). And God is often portrayed as a good shepherd, watching over his flock in the same way (Ps 1:6, Ps 121:8, Jer 31:10). Most of us can recite the first line of Psalm 23 from the King James Version, "The Lord is my shepherd, I shall not want." The NIV offers a different translation, "I lack nothing," but it just does not convey the same level of comfort or warmth to me. "I shall not want" because the good shepherd cares so deeply for me. And Jesus said, "I am the good shepherd, I know my sheep and my sheep know me—just as the Father knows me and I know the Father—and I lay down life for the sheep" (John 10:14–25). What else is there to want when we have a shepherd like that watching over us?

A fourth way that watching is used in Scripture means *to be careful*, to take note, to be prudent. Jesus told Peter and the sons of Zebedee, James and John, to "Watch and pray so that you will not fall into temptation. The spirit is willing, but the flesh is weak" (Matt 26:41). Certainly, if you know that about the flesh, it is good to pray—and to be careful. In a similar vein, Paul cautioned his young colleague, Timothy, "Watch your life and doctrine closely" (1 Tim 4:16). That's good advice for all of us. Watch your life, be careful, take note, and be prudent. And that goes for your doctrine, too. It is important, so be careful with it. Watch how you live. Take care of your reputation. Keep your word. Live wisely. Watch.

We see from Scripture that watching and waiting are both associated intimately with holy silence. In fact, they are practices that can help establish and sustain the habit of holy silence in your life. Let's look at some concrete ways to cultivate this helpful habit.

Some Practical Advice

Perhaps the first thing to note is that the habit of holy silence *is* a habit. Holy silence doesn't come naturally to most of us. We have to work at it intentionally, and when we do, we get better at it. It becomes a habit, a good habit.

To help you get into the practice of holy silence, try putting away your technology for a part of each day and for one day each month. You may have to make an appointment with yourself to do so. That's quite all right. The point is to make time without distraction, time to wait and watch, to listen to your life and to God.

Learn to listen. Listening is a skill, and like any skill, you get better at it with practice. Take a "listening walk" in your neighborhood. See what you hear. And if you see a neighbor, ask them questions—and listen. Don't talk about yourself. Be intentional about hearing as much as you can while saying as little as possible. Your friends may ask you if you're feeling okay. Tell them, "Sure, I'm just cultivating the habit of holy silence." Well, maybe it would be better to just say that you are on a listening mission or something like that. There is no need to scare anyone away. Be an intentional listener.

Focus on holy silence when you pray. For most of us, praying means words, our words. Set aside ten minutes each day to pray by listening. Start by asking this simple question, "Lord, please speak into my life. I'm listening." Then, wait and watch, practicing holy silence. I believe that God will honor your prayers, speaking to you in any variety of ways. When it is clear that God is speaking to you, then follow the instructions. It's honestly that simple.

Don't practice or permit unholy silence in your family. Much like curbing gossip, you can start by refraining from using it yourself. Carefully and prayerfully examine your life to see if that nasty habit has crept in and taken root. If it has, you have to pull that weed quickly. And don't allow unholy silence to be practiced in your presence either. We all know that it is hurtful. If we stand by in silence and let others be marginalized or punished with silence, our silence is less than holy, too.

Conclusion

In this chapter, we started with the admission that not all silence is holy, and described several forms of this nasty weed. Then, we explored three formative practices that will help us cultivate the habit of holy silence: keeping quiet, being present, and listening. Next, we consulted Scripture, looking at two spiritual activities that are closely associated with holy silence: waiting and watching. Finally, we offered five practical ways to begin the cultivation of the habit of holy silence: make it a daily practice, put away your technology on a regular basis, take a listening walk in your neighborhood, pray without words, and don't allow unholy silence to take root in your family.

As we conclude this chapter, I must admit that this is one of the hardest spiritual disciplines for me, and I would suppose for many of us. In our self-centered, noisy lives, purposely making and taking time to listen to God and to others is, sadly, spiritually countercultural. We are a generation of doers, and we have not been taught how to listen. It is time to change the culture, starting right where we live.

Questions for Discussion and Reflection

1. What forms of unholy silence are practiced in your family or workplace?

2. What is the biggest impediment to the practice of holy silence for you? What can you do about it?

3. Do you have a time and place for solitude each day, disconnected from all forms of communication technology?

4. Do you take time each day to pray without words, to listen to God? If not, how could you make this practice a reality?

5. How do you know when God is speaking to you? How has God revealed himself to you in recent days?

I will try this day to live a simple, sincere, and serene life, repelling promptly every thought of discontent, anxiety, discouragement, impurity, and self-seeking; cultivating cheerfulness, magnanimity, charity, and the habit of holy silence . . .

— PART III —

Exercising Graceful Activities

Economy, Diligence, Fidelity, and Faith

IN PART I, WE started by working on repelling different forms of negativity that can choke our spiritual gardens, pulling weeds, if you will; and in Part II, we explored ways to cultivate and nourish a set of positive attitudes that will provide a fertile soil for spiritual growth. Now in Part III, we will consider some elements of a sincere life by examining a set of grace-filled activities that bring substance and character to our spiritual walk: economy in expenditure, diligence in appointed service, fidelity to every trust, and a childlike faith in God. These four disciplines will engender genuine peace and harmony, some of the first fruits from a flourishing spiritual garden.

You will note that this section of our daily prayer, "A Morning Resolve," also contains two additional activities: generosity in giving and carefulness in conversation. Of course, these are important, formative activities, too, but we have already discussed them in detail in earlier chapters. As my father would say, "There's no need to repeat the obvious." While I didn't always like all the advice my dad would send my way, I think, in this case, he was right. He usually was.

— 10 —

Economy in Expenditure

You have succeeded in life when all you really want is only what you really need.

—*VERNON HOWARD*

Introduction

I DON'T WANT THIS chapter to read like a section borrowed from a local community college personal finance course, but exercising economy in expenditure has a lot to do with our spending. What we will do to get money, what money means to us, and what we do with it says much about our values and our commitments. It provides a glimpse into the priorities by which we live and the dreams for which we live. Moreover, it indicates how we understand the kingdom—and who rules it. So, as it turns out, spending money wisely is a spiritual practice. In this chapter, we will look at several behaviors and values that I trust will help us sort out some of the havoc that unexamined and uncontrolled spending can bring into our lives, and provide a way forward as we pray this week to exercise economy in expenditure. I am convinced that it is a learned behavior, and it is one of the primary keys to living a simple, sincere, and serene life.

Before we start, I want to be clear that I know that examining the practice of economy in expenditure is a complex subject, a very personal subject, and it is fraught with difficulties because it reveals and critiques some of our most profound commitments and deeply held beliefs. Spending money is both a tangible and a symbolic activity, and there is no simple "one correct approach" to the way we order our resources. There are some who advocate an extremely rigid approach to the use of money, and others have become very popular promoting the "Christian" way, outlining God's intention for us. While I honestly believe that their systems can be effective, I get nervous when I hear that it is *the* Christian way or the only way to think about spending. I believe we have been given a great deal of freedom in this life, and good minds, too. We should use both. God calls us to be wise followers, not robots.

I also know that this topic can bring to light issues of abuse, mistreatment, and downright meanness. Particularly in families, who controls the finances and how that control is maintained can become an ugly, mean-spirited, hurtful use of power. So if this chapter brings up wounds or deep-seeded anger, I urge you to seek out someone to talk to—a trusted friend, a spiritual director, or a professional. Don't go it alone.

With these framing comments made, let's look at four aspects of spending that will help us navigate our way safely through this minefield: distinguishing between wants and needs, recognizing the purchase buzz, practicing patience, and exercising prudence.

Wants and Needs

A need is something that you have to have. A want is something you would like to have. Most of us honestly know the difference, but oh how our minds can rationalize once we begin shopping in a store or online. All of a sudden, you really need that pair of shoes, or that tool, or that new phone. Do you? Really? And strangely, most often the person that you are working to convince is you! We develop the strange habit of arguing with ourselves, and winning the argument. We give in to our own skills of persuasion. What if we consistently made it a practice to query ourselves before most purchases with these questions: "Is this really a need or just a want? Do I have the funds to purchase it? If so, is this the best way to use my discretionary funds? Is this the best time to purchase? Are there other things that should come first? Would this purchase diminish or delay other commitments that I have made?" Please don't take this as an indictment against purchasing things that you want. It is not. Honestly, I see nothing inherently wrong with buying things that you want in addition to the things that you need (with discretion, of course). But I am suggesting that it is important to be thoughtful and discerning about all your purchases.

And wouldn't it be helpful if churches would use the same discernment process to distinguish between wants and needs, too? There are so many reports of conflict as churches try to develop realistic operating budgets. Even in the healthiest churches, there are just too many good ideas and not enough dollars. To order or reorder priorities, distinguishing between wants and needs is a good place to start.

In addition to distinguishing between wants and needs, it is helpful to reflect on why a particular "want" is so important to you, so compelling. What is the message behind the purchase? Let me illustrate. When I was in the sixth grade, I would do some extra chores around the house to get a little spending money for a pack of baseball cards or some penny candy. On one occasion, I took my fifty cents to the grocery store and bought a loaf of "store-bought" bread, the one with the balloons on the wrapper. The slices were thin and wonderfully uniform. I couldn't wait to make a sandwich to take to school instead of using my mom's homemade bread. Her slices were too thick, I thought, making my sandwich look ugly. Of course, right now I would give a lot more than fifty cents to have a loaf of my mother's homemade bread, and I can't even imagine trading it for some store-bought bread. So, why was it so important to me to have a sandwich that looked store-bought? Because I wanted to be like my classmates, I wanted to fit in. Obviously, even at a very early age, I had the notion that to be included, to be okay, I had to have certain things and look a certain way. The store-bought bread had social significance, and so did my mom's bread. One meant that I was cool; the other meant that I was poor.

Evidently, when I watched cowboy movies on Saturday morning, I took away more than just the thrill of seeing the bad guys brought to justice. I also received messages that shaped how I perceived my circumstances, and told me what I could do to make them better. Honestly, this is a bit disturbing for two reasons. First, that kind of advertising aimed at children seems unfair. After all, children are not as able to step back and reflect on all the messages that come their way. They are shaped without their knowledge or consent. It is so important for adults to teach children to be thoughtful, reflective consumers, and to model that behavior for them. Second, it is disturbing because I am still influenced by those same messages even though I believe that I am a thoughtful, reflective adult. We, all of us, are bombarded by messages all the time from everywhere. And most of us lack the inclination and insight to step back and think carefully about all that is going on when we are so eager to make a purchase. It is one thing to clarify our wants from our needs. It is an entirely different thing to step away from all this trivial noise and consciously work to understand what is going on that makes the things we want so much seem so necessary. We have not been conditioned or taught to do this well, but it can be learned—and it will bring clarity to our spending and serenity to our lives.

The Purchase Buzz

I have to admit that I do like to buy things. When I buy a new jacket or something for the kitchen, it makes me feel good. I get a purchase buzz. And as far as I am concerned, there is nothing wrong with feeling good about a wise purchase. Shopping can be fun! The problem comes when we expect more from our shopping than the goods can or should deliver. I remember asking my mother for a pair of Red Ball Jets for my birthday. According to the commercials, they would make me "run faster, jump higher, and last longer." Who couldn't use that? I was so excited as I laced up my new sneakers for the first time. I raced into the backyard and jumped as high as I could. It was a good jump, but it honestly didn't seem to be any higher than before. I reckoned that it would take time for the shoes to break in. But by the end of the day, I came to the realization that I wasn't running faster or jumping higher, and my stamina hadn't improved either. I learned a painful lesson that day: don't believe everything that is told to you by someone who wants to sell you something, or as my mom would put it, "Things aren't always what they're cracked up to be." Of course, she was right.

It is also important to recognize that there's a shelf life for a purchase buzz. With use, things become more commonplace and the buzz fades. This is as it should be, but when we think that having a purchase buzz is normal—and necessary—we get into difficulties. When that happens, we need another purchase, then another, and then another to sustain the buzz. Sadly, there's no end to this circle dance, and over time the buying becomes less satisfying and sadly addictive. We were not created to live by buzz along.

Patience

We are not a patient lot. I recently heard someone say that if he didn't hurry and preorder a new model of a particular phone, it might take six weeks to get one. Who can wait! Seriously, is six weeks really too long to wait, particularly for a new model of a phone when your current version is working just fine? Who knows, with patience you might even be able to wait a week or two longer! For a good deal of technology, my motto is: If it isn't broke, don't upgrade it.

In our economy, however, we don't need to have patience. No, we have credit. For many purchases, we really do not even know the full cost of the purchase, just the size of the monthly payments. As long as we can make the payments, all is well. Right? Well, maybe. I am not one to argue that you should never borrow. There are times when it makes sense to me, particularly when the cost of borrowing is low and the return on the investment is high. For example, borrowing to buy a home or to invest in higher education can be a wise course of action. I fear that those who argue that you should never borrow, not even to attend a Christian college or university, miss the point. I would agree that if you are only after a credential, then there are plenty of places to earn one that is much less expensive. However, if you are looking to prepare for a lifetime of faithful living, then borrowing for the opportunity to embrace a formative, life-directing educational experience can be worth every penny, perhaps the wisest investment you will ever make. The key, it seems to me, is to be a careful investor not only with your money, but with your entire life, too. There is no doubt that holding strictly to prohibitions about borrowing will, in the short run, save you some money. But if the "never borrow" rule keeps you or your family from pivotal, life-shaping experiences, there are real losses to be acknowledged, too. We are called to live a full life, not just survive it.

With that being said, let me be clear. Borrowing can also be dangerous and damaging—both economically and spiritually. When we borrow and buy because we do not have the patience to wait or the discipline to save, we burden our futures, often in disastrous ways. When we carry heavy debt we gamble that our economic future will remain the same or get better. Since the economic collapse of 2008, we know that this is not always the case. With all borrowing, there should be an exit strategy. What will you do if your economic situation changes?

Perhaps the biggest culprit that propels our no patience-no worries culture is the credit card—or for many of us, credit cards. They are easy to obtain, easy to use, and easy to stay in good standing with minimal payments—but at a horrific financial cost. The interest rates charged when you fail to pay off the credit card balance each month are staggering, and a maxed out card, particularly due to a litany of nonessential purchases, weighs down both your pocketbook and your spirit like an anchor. It often takes years to recover, and the damage done to family and self is real. When we pray to learn how to exercise economy in expenditure, it is, in large part, a prayer for patience.

Prudence

To exercise prudence means to use good judgment, common sense, caution, and wisdom. It is easy to see that prudence has a great deal to do with economy in expenditure. In our lifetime, we will purchase many goods and services and spend money on a variety of things—entertainment, travel, family outings, etc. This is fine. There is no need to live as a miser. The key is to be a wise, careful consumer, one who uses good judgment and common sense. In most cases, it is common sense to abstain from buying things you do not need with money you do not have.

It is also prudent to reuse, recycle, and repair whenever we can. Many things we buy have a limited shelf life, planned obsolescence. Things will wear out. When they do, there is wisdom in looking at all the options before racing to the store to buy a new one. And when we do purchase, there may be wisdom in spending a bit more for quality, quality that will last. The cheapest item isn't always the best purchase. We will have more to say about prudence in the section Some Practical Advice. Suffice it here to say that swimming in deep water and drowning are not the same thing. Spending and wasting money are not the same thing either. The difference is using good judgment and common sense. Unfortunately, common sense is not always that common.

Scripture

On several occasions in this book, I have argued that God's economy is different, guided by different values, kingdom values. And if we live by kingdom values, we will act differently. This is so very true when it comes to the way we spend money. Our dominant cultural values are appearance, achievement, and affluence, and the driving message we hear in so much of today's marketing is that money helps us accomplish these ends. That is to say, money makes us look better, demonstrates our attainments, and lets everyone know that we are flourishing. The more we spend, the more successful we are.

In God's economy, the driving values are character, compassion, and community—the three C's. I contend that if our lives are guided by the three C's, we will understand spending differently. In Matthew 20, Jesus tells the parable of the Workers in the Vineyard. Essentially, the owner of the vineyard hires some workers for the day and they go to work. Throughout the day, the owner continues to bring on workers, some hired very late in the day. As evening approaches, the landlord pays everyone a full day's wage, even though some worked only a few hours. Those who were hired late in the day were obviously thrilled, but the workers who put in a full day were angry. "It isn't fair," they protested. "We worked longer for the same pay." And in one sense, they were correct. If their pay was to be based on what time they put in, then they had every right to feel that they had been cheated. But in God's economy, it is not about getting what you deserve, but about receiving more than you can possibly imagine. In God's economy, it is about generosity and grace. What if graceful generosity, guided by character, compassion, and community, shaped our getting and spending? I believe that it would bring a deeper understanding and direction to our practice of economy in expenditure.

Some Practical Advice

Before we close this chapter, let me offer some very practical words of advice for prudent and patient spending. None of these suggestions are earth-shaking, but they will have a tangible and cumulative effect if practiced faithfully.

Be a Thoughtful Consumer

There are three things you can do to spend wisely. First, take time to analyze the commercials and other means of marketing that come your way. What messages are being communicated? Do they align with kingdom values? And if you have children, teach them to do the same. Critiquing the messages rather than passively receiving them is a learned but prudent discipline, and you get better with practice. Second, work to differentiate between needs and wants, and do not let others differentiate them for you. I recently heard a marketing professional say, "My job is to make people think they need things that they don't even know they want." This is dangerous. Third, recognize the purchase buzz for what it is—and what it isn't. It can be an enjoyable add-on to a wise purchase, but it does not last very long. Don't come to expect that the purpose of shopping is to provide the buzz. If you do, you are headed for trouble.

Live within Your Means

I can't think of anything more impressive or more important to living a serene life than to live happily within your means. Spending money you don't have on things you don't need can lead to many things, but dignity and independence are not two of them. Keep a very low credit limit on your credit card, and pay it off monthly. One of the most important spiritual disciplines you can undertake is to create a weekly or monthly financial budget and follow it faithfully. It brings dignity and independence, and reduces stress and frustration, some of the fruits of a simple, sincere, and serene life.

Put Something Away Each Month

Regardless of the size of your monthly income, put something away each month for savings and for charity/church—and don't talk yourself into spending it on something else. Even if it is only five dollars each month, get into the practice of saving and giving. Living within your means does not mean that you spend everything you bring in. Over time, this will become a healthy habit as you practice kingdom values.

Conclusion

The key to practicing economy in expenditure is to keep first things first. It is not living as a miser—that is poverty, not serenity. Rather, it is living with a healthy set of priorities. As we have discussed in this chapter, this involves being a thoughtful and discriminating consumer, living within your means, exercising patience and prudence, and ordering your spending by kingdom values. How we spend our money says a great deal about us. May those who watch our lives find us faithful participants in God's economy.

Questions for Discussion and Reflection

1. What kinds of advertising influence you the most? Think of an ad that pushes your "purchase now" or "I really want that" button. Why do you think it does that?

2. Most of us from time to time convince ourselves that a want is really a need. When was the last time you had that conversation with yourself, and if you gave in, what did you buy? Any regrets?

3. What is your philosophy about credit and the use of credit cards? How are you managing your debt wisely?

4. In this chapter, I suggested that character, compassion, and community are kingdom values. How could this align or realign your spending priorities?

5. Can you think of a time when you were either impatient or imprudent with a purchase? What was the result and what is to be learned from that experience?

I will try this day to live a simple, sincere, and serene life, repelling promptly every thought of discontent, anxiety, discouragement, impurity, and self-seeking; cultivating cheerfulness, magnanimity, charity, and the habit of holy silence; exercising economy in expenditure . . .

— 11 —

Diligence in Appointed Service

Every job is a portrait of the person who does it. Autograph your work with excellence.

—ABRAHAM LINCOLN

Introduction

WHEN I FIRST HEARD the phrase "diligence in appointed service," I must confess that it made me think of what I call "dog work." You know, the kind of work that is passed down to you without consultation or consent, assignments that you are obligated to do but bring very little joy to your spirit. To be honest, no one I know likes dog work but we all have to lean in and do it occasionally. That's part of life. Fortunately, this is not a chapter on the spiritual discipline of doing things you dislike. Rather, in this chapter we will explore what it means to find meaning in our appointed tasks, and how to embrace the deep spiritual value found in service to others. In this chapter, we will pray that we will exercise diligence in appointed service. Let's begin!

Diligence in Appointed Service

Let's start with diligence, most often defined as careful and persistent work or effort. As Abraham Lincoln knew, your work becomes your autograph. It means something. How you go about your appointed service tells others who you are, for better or worse. For me, it starts by just showing up—early. As a boy, I could not understand why my dad would insist on being at work at 6:30 AM when the workday didn't start until 7:00. Wasn't 6:58 close enough? For him, the answer was clearly "no." There are plenty of coaches who teach their players that if your arrive for a 3:00 practice at 2:55, you are already ten minutes late. And one corporate executive in the aircraft industry lamented to me that she wished her employees were as diligent about arriving for work on time as they were about leaving for lunch or clocking out for the weekend. So, clearly your work habits say something about you, and showing up early has a very practical dimension, too. When you arrive early, you have time to talk to others in a less work-focused, unhurried way, and time to thoughtfully and carefully plan out your day or the next meeting. I honestly believe that it makes your work more productive and enjoyable. Your autograph begins by showing up early.

Diligence also means showing up every day. If you say you will be there to help out, then be there. When friends and colleagues can't count on you to do what you say you will do, you are in spiritual trouble. Running around apologizing for missing the work project, the rehearsal, the service, the outing, or the youth activity gets very old very quickly. At the least, it is a terrible habit, and after awhile, you lose credibility and influence. And it's about the surest way I know to lose your job, too.

Also, the practice of diligence means that you get today's work done today. When you think about it, you really only have two days—today, this day, and tomorrow, that day. To be diligent, you focus on this day, not that day, getting what needs to be done today no matter how attractive and seductive it seems to wait until later. Gardens do not just magically appear in full bloom. No, gardens flourish with persistent attention, care, and hard work—whether the garden is spiritual or in your backyard. Spring work can't wait for warmer weather in June.

To be clear, however, diligence involves more than just showing up—even early and often, as important as these habits are. Diligence also involves careful and persistent work and effort. In other words, after you show up, you do your very best work. You want your signature to be meticulous, watchful, and thorough work. No shortcuts. And I've found that when I don't think I have the time to do a task right the first time, I have to find the time to do it over again. Avoidable do-overs are not an attractive personal signature. But, you may be thinking, what does all of this have to do with spiritual growth, with cultivating a flourishing spiritual garden?

Isn't this just a good work ethic? The answer is yes, care and persistence are part of a strong work ethic, but I believe there is much more to it than that. The way you approach your work not only says something about you, it also shapes you. And it is a way to embrace the world and make your way through it as a faithful presence, as a testimony, if you will. Am I saying that there is a spiritual aspect to the way we approach work? Yes! I believe that your work can be a thin place, a place where the physical and spiritual worlds are both evident. Now, if this sounds a bit too mystical, I apologize, but I truly believe there are implications for the way we carry out our duties that extend far beyond the immediate. Exercising diligence is a spiritual act.

Diligence in *Appointed* Service

We are praying this week to learn to exercise diligence in appointed service. Synonyms for *appointed* give you the range of ways this word can be understood and used: *assigned, prescribed, prearranged, chosen, selected*, and *ordained*. Let's look at three aspects of "appointed" service that could use some amplification. First, there is a big difference between volunteering for a task (you actually say that you will do it) and being voluntold (being volunteered for an assignment without your knowledge or approval, or being asked in such a way that you really can't say no). I've experienced both. Once the president of the university asked me to volunteer to lead a very controversial taskforce on campus, but he asked me in a public meeting with all the faculty and trustees in attendance right after he had given a speech on the great need for individuals to step up and help out when asked. I said yes, but I really couldn't say no. I was voluntold.

On another occasion, I attended a banquet honoring a friend. Imagine my surprise when I read the evening's program and found out that I was the main speaker—and I didn't know it! Again, I was voluntold. I bring up the issue of voluntelling because it is far too prevalent in so many families, churches, and organizations. It drains the spirit. No one likes to be manipulated, strong-armed, or embarrassed. Voluntelling does all three. It is not a spiritual practice that bears good fruit. It undermines the spirit of volunteerism and gives you good reason to stay away when, in fact, your gifts, skills, and abilities are so very much needed.

Just as there is a crucial distinction between volunteering and voluntelling, there is also a critical difference between being appointed and being anointed. In many instances, the leader of an organization or group is chosen, selected, or elected. In particular, most churches, universities, and civic organizations go to great lengths to establish detailed protocols and procedures for the election or appointment of leaders. This is as it should be. I've seen more than one organization get into hot water because they didn't have good selection protocols in place, or more often than not, they didn't follow the protocols they had. I have come to believe that the careful and faithful selection or appointment of leadership is a spiritual practice, even in secular settings.

The flip side of the coin occurs when leaders, no matter how well the selection process was conceived and completed, confuse being appointed with being anointed. That is to say, they forget that they are in that position to serve the common good. They begin to conceive of their position as a personal reward or a gift from God. Appointed leadership that turns into anointed leadership almost always goes sideways, and people and organizations suffer. After all, if the leader views the organization as a personal possession or believes that it is their God-given right to lead, then why would that leader need to listen to anyone else? In fact, if someone does not agree with the direction set, they must not be in tune with God. Right? In essence, they must go—and they usually do. Given all the troubles we see in our churches, if voluntelling is a negative practice, then anointed leadership is downright hurtful—and dangerous.

Fortunately, appointed service has many positive dimensions, too. One of the best ways to understand appointed service is to think of it in terms of vocation. From the Latin, *vocatio* means a call or summons. Thus, if you see your appointed service as a calling, whether it be in a position of leadership or cleaning up after the service, it is your vocation—a call from God to use your gifts, abilities, and opportunities for the kingdom, not in self-service or promotion. However appointed, selected, or elected, humility is the key ingredient, the rich soil for leadership and functionality. Accepting your assignment as a summons to serve in the kingdom rather than as a personal gift from God to feather your own kingdom keeps the task in proper perspective. And where is the best place to find your vocation? Look at the intersection of your abilities and your opportunities. That's a wonderful starting place.

Diligence in Appointed *Service*

Thus far, we have examined two words: *diligence* and *appointed*. Before we put the phrase back together and look at Scripture and some practical advice, let's talk just a brief moment about service. I think we all agree that it is a good thing. No one is against it. The expectation that you will do some service is a common aspect in most professions. For example, when a university professor in the US is evaluated for promotion, say from Assistant Professor to Associate Professor, the process will include an examination of three elements: teaching, research, and service. It is recognized that being a professor means giving something back, using one's knowledge and skills for the common good. Having received much in the way of training and support (we all stand on the shoulders of those who came before us), service is an intentional aspect of professional life. In this case, service is a civil expectation.

Service is a spiritual discipline, too, part of our prayer to exercise *diligence in appointed service*. Service is not just an add-on, something we do if you have some spare time. No, giving back through service is the rent you pay for living on this earth. It is an essential aspect of being a faithful presence where you live and work. I like to think of service as part of a tithe, something that belongs to God. It improves the quality of life of those around you and lifts your own spirits, too. And it shapes you in wonderful and unexpected ways, particularly when service is approached as an expression of love rather than a duty to be performed. All this to say, when you are asked or appointed to a position of service, it is truly a high calling. When you volunteer (rather than being voluntold) for a position of service, it can be a tangible way for your calling or summons to be seen and heard. If you are diligent in that task, God is honored, others are helped, and you are shaped and formed. And if nurtured in the rich soil of humility, your spiritual garden will bear good fruit.

Scripture

Throughout Scripture, there are stories of those who did not perform their appointed service with diligence. Jonah comes quickly to mind. God called him to a very specific assignment. He was to deliver a message to the people of Nineveh, telling them to repent and turn from their wicked ways or God would destroy them. At first, he didn't want to go and preach to his nation's longtime enemy, so he ran away instead. But he soon changed his mind. Funny, it seems that spending three days in the belly of a great fish gave him plenty of time to reflect on the consequences of his decisions. So, when he reached dry land, Jonah went and preached repentance to the Ninevites. Much to his surprise they listened to him and repented. And even more shocking to Jonah, God listened to their prayers and relented. He took compassion on them and did not destroy their city—and this made Jonah mad! Obviously, this is not a model of diligence in appointed service.

King Saul also comes to mind. Certainly, he is not a poster child for servant leadership. His ego clouded his judgment, and along the way he forgot that he was appointed to serve the people. Instead, everything he did was designed to preserve and perpetuate his own power and reputation, including trying to get rid of all those who could be a threat—even those who were actually truly loyal to him, such as David. King Saul confused appointed and anointed leadership, and service to the greater good was the last thing he had in mind. No diligence in appointed service here.

Of course, there are many positive examples in Scripture, too. Think of Mary, the mother of Jesus. Certainly she was faithful to an astonishing, almost unbelievable summons, willing to risk her reputation and standing in the community, not to mention her own health and welfare. In the face of all of this, she said, "I am the Lord's servant. May your word to me be fulfilled" (Luke 1:38). And Abraham, who when called to go to a strange, new land, "obeyed and went, even though he did not know where he was going" (Heb 11:8). Paul was dogged in his response to the assignment he received on the Damascus Road. As he wrote to Timothy, "I have fought the good fight, I have finished the race, I have kept the faith" (2 Tim 4:7). And there are so many more that I could list: Mary and Martha, the sisters close to Jesus, Sarah, Rahab, Elizabeth, the mother of John the Baptist, and John the Baptist himself. Surely, they were all models of diligence to appointed service, accepting their vocation to be a faithful presence where they were—and they found themselves is some remarkable places and circumstances, not all of them happy ones.

There are also examples of those who were faithful to their call—well, at least most of the time. I think of King David, who wrote so many of our favorite Psalms expressing his deep faith and devotion to God, but came up short when he saw Beersheba and decided to make her his queen, disregarding the uncomfortable fact that she was married to someone else. And Peter, the rock and builder of the church, who tried to protect Jesus on the night he was arrested by wildly swinging his sword, separating a servant from his ear. Then, Peter denied that he even knew Christ three times before the sun came up the next morning. Honestly, I think most of us fall into the "mostly faithful" crowd, too. I like to say that we're all cracked pots. Thank God for grace and forgiveness.

One of the finest examples of diligence in appointed service in Scripture is found in the Old Testament book of Nehemiah, a story of . . . who else, Nehemiah! He was a cupbearer for the king of Babylon, Artaxerxes. He had a great job, but when he heard that the walls of Jerusalem were in ruins, it moved him greatly (he wept) and he knew that he had to do something about it. He had discovered his vocation, or perhaps his vocation had summoned him. He would rebuild the walls of Jerusalem. And he did. He volunteered for the job, received official sponsorship from the king (he went through proper channels), carefully planned the task at hand, organized and rallied the workers to put forth extraordinary effort, and rebuilt the walls and gates of the city. He was truly diligent in appointed service. Well done!

Yes, well done, indeed, but there is much more to the story. First, it is important to point out that just because Nehemiah went through the proper channels, carefully and strategically organizing and planning the project and leading effectively, it didn't mean that all went smoothly. In fact, he faced serious and malicious opposition. He received death threats, and the laborers had to carry a sword in one hand and their tools in the other. Jealous people (those who found themselves on the outside or their current positions diminished) worked to undermine his best efforts. It got nasty. It is important to remember that doing things the right away will not always guarantee smooth sailing. It's the right thing to do, of course, but don't be surprised if you encounter an unhealthy undercurrent at work, even in the church. Leading is hard work.

The other intriguing aspect of this story is that Nehemiah's vocation or summons somehow expanded into something far more than he expected. He felt compelled to go back to Jerusalem and rebuild the walls, but he ended up rebuilding much more than that. After the walls were up, he could have returned to his cushy cupbearer job with the king of Babylon. Job done—time to go. Rather, he stayed on in Jerusalem and rebuilt the community, too, restoring order, caring for the poor, restocking the storehouses, and bringing back the exiles. It is a marvelous story of God's grace. Nehemiah responded to the call to rebuild the walls, but the end result was social and spiritual renewal. In so many times and ways, when you respond to God's summons, you can only see the tip of the iceberg of God's intentions and the possibilities that lie ahead. We are only called to be faithful. The rest is grace.

And I would be remiss if I didn't point out the obvious—the best example of exercising diligence in appointed service found in Scripture is Jesus. Being fully human, he had no desire for a painful death. He was full of life and hope and promise. Jesus took some of his trusted friends and went to a place called Gethsemane. He prayed fervently to his father, "If it is possible, may this cup be taken from me." What an amazingly honest prayer. But even more amazing, he quickly and quietly added, "Yet not as I will, but as you will" (Matt 26:39). Diligence in appointed service to the point of death on the cross; it is truly a remarkable story. And three days later, we see that just as in the case of rebuilding the walls with Nehemiah, the cross was not the end of the story for Jesus—not even close. The rest is grace.

Some Practical Advice

The first bit of practical advice that I would offer is this: take your vocation seriously. That is to say, realize and appreciate that the gifts, abilities, and opportunities that you have are not there by some random chance, but rather by grace. And in fact, your gifts are a form of grace to others. Peter, the apostle of Christ, puts it this way: "Each of you should use whatever gift you have received to serve others, as faithful stewards of God's grace in its various forms" (1 Pet 4:10). So, being a faithful steward of God's grace *is* your calling. In fact, it feels more like a summons to me: Know your gifts; use your gifts.

Second, autograph your work with diligence and excellence. Whatever you are called to do, bring your very best effort and organization to the task. It should be just as hard to think of mediocre effort as it is to think of mediocre grace. Is anyone interested in just so-so grace? I'm not, to be sure. When we consider that our service to others is a form of God's grace, how can we settle for anything less than doing our very best? And doing your best work can become a very helpful, positive habit. All it takes is consistent practice.

Third, take stock of the service possibilities that exist in your everyday life. No need to look for heroic opportunities. Just look around your own neighborhood, school, or church. And if you consider service as an important and necessary aspect of who you are, it won't just be an add-on. It is the stuff of life together.

Fourth, and this is a hard one, lose yourself in humility. One of the hardest things to do in life is to step back or step aside and not pursue the limelight. For most of us, it takes work because we have learned to enjoy recognition. It makes us feel good about ourselves. It is much harder to unlearn, but it can be done if you are intentional about it. In fact, it can be a formative practice.

Fifth, if you are diligent in appointed service, don't be surprised when adversity rears its ugly head. Doing things the right way doesn't guarantee smooth sailing. People can be mean-spirited, jealous, and self-serving. Being faithful has it own rewards, to be sure, but an easy go isn't one of them. So, go in with your eyes wide open. I wonder if this is what Jesus meant when he told his disciples, "Go! I am sending you out like lambs among wolves" (Luke 10:3). Be a lamb, but watch out for the wolves, too.

Before we close this section on practical advice, there is one final piece of advice about being diligent. As important as it is to be diligent, it is just as important to know when to walk away. I realize that this may seem to be contradictory to everything that has been written heretofore, but I don't think it is. There may be times when you simply cannot do what you are called to do, or others will not let you, or in attending to the task, you put your physical or emotional or spiritual well-being at risk. When you recognize that you are facing that situation, hit the reset button and walk away. There will be other days. It is good to recognize when it is simply a matter of extra work and persistence to swim upstream. When it is, then swim harder. But if you are swimming up a toxic stream, then no amount of effort is worth the harm done to you and to others. Get out of the toxic stream and find healthier waters.

Conclusion

In this chapter, we have examined the meaning of diligence, autographing your work with excellence; the meaning of being summoned or appointed as opposed to being anointed; and the meaning of service, understanding it as a lifelong tithe rather than an add-on we do once a month for charity. We looked closely at the story of Nehemiah, a wonderful story of diligence in appointed service, and noticed that there is often more to a calling than we could ever expect or possibly anticipate. And we closed the chapter with some practical advice for putting diligence in appointed service into practice, including the possibility that there may be times when the proper course of action is to walk away and look for other times and places to serve.

In the last analysis, it is important to understand that being diligent in appointed service is actually grace at work. It is a divine mystery, and a spiritual practice that will bear good fruit in season.

Questions for Discussion and Reflection

1. How would you describe your calling, your vocation?

2. What do you see as the implications for thinking of your vocation as a summons rather than a calling?

3. It is easy to talk about excellence, but sometimes hard to put it into practice. How would you define excellence in your daily work? Are there concrete steps you could take to improve your approach to the tasks at hand?

4. There has been much written about servant leadership, but much less about servant followership. What are three things that you could do to assist someone else as they attempt to be diligent in their appointed service? How can you be a better follower?

5. If you face adversity in appointed service, how would you know when to "keep your oars in the water" and when to "hit the reset button" and walk away? What would make a place of service truly toxic for you?

I will try this day to live a simple, sincere, and serene life, repelling promptly every thought of discontent, anxiety, discouragement, impurity, and self-seeking; cultivating cheerfulness, magnanimity, charity, and the habit of holy silence; exercising economy in expenditure, generosity in giving, carefulness in conversation, diligence in appointed service . . .

Fidelity to Every Trust

I do not pray for success. I ask for faithfulness.

—MOTHER TERESA

Introduction

What does it mean to exercise fidelity to every trust, and how do we do it? In this chapter, we will examine the meaning of fidelity and trust, and we will consider that little word in between—*every*. As it turns out, it is a very important little word, and it has a great deal to do with credibility.

Credibility

Let's think about the idea of credibility a bit by looking at two old family stories. The first story is about Jack, a backwoodsman in almost every respect. He was an excellent fishing and hunting guide, knew how to live off the land, and, of course, wore a thick, black beard. Oh, and he chewed tobacco, too. He was shy and uncomfortable in public, preferring the woods and waters to communities and crowds. He was one of my father's best friends. Dad and Jack would canoe, camp, and sit for hours talking about diesel engines and telling stories about hunting wild animals and catching huge fish, and I have no doubt that most of them were true—at least to some extent.

One day, my father called Jack and told him that he had been diagnosed with colon cancer, and would be going in for surgery the next week. Jack asked when the surgery was scheduled, and my father said that he didn't rightly recall, but knew that he would have to go in very early on that day. Jack said that he would be there for support. My father protested. You see, Jack lived on a lake about twenty miles from the nearest paved road, and it was a good sixteen-hour drive from that paved road to the hospital where the surgery would take place. Dad said it would be more than sufficient if Jack would simply remember him with a prayer on the day in question.

My father and mother arrived at the hospital at 4:30 AM on the day of the surgery. Jack met them in the parking lot with a grin. "I didn't know what time you would be arriving, but I knew you well enough to know that you would be early," Jack told Dad. "So, I arrived here about midnight and have been here waiting for you." In an unusual show of emotion, they hugged. Jack waited there in the parking lot all day until word came late in the afternoon that the surgery had been successful. He didn't even leave for lunch. Then, he said goodbye to my mother, climbed back into his pickup, and headed back home. He said that he would call my dad in a few days to see how he was doing, and he did.

The other friend story is about Alice. She was a sweet, outgoing, caring person. She would do anything for you if she could, and was an active member in our local church. Whenever a request was made for help at the church, with the choir, with the youth group, in the food pantry, or in the social hall, Alice was the first to volunteer. Her name was always at the top of the list. You could count on that. You could also count on that on more occasions than not, Alice would be a no-show. Later that week, you would receive a mournful phone call. Alice would be in tears—apologizing for the fact that she had forgotten or that something else came up, and asking for forgiveness. And she would always follow up the phone call with a note of apology, too, begging for forgiveness again. I often wondered if she would save time by having a preprinted stock of such cards on hand. It happened so often that when Alice's name appeared on the volunteer list, it was simply ignored. And after a while, the calls for forgiveness became an irritation, too. Somehow, it always ended up being about Alice and her very busy life. At best, it was a tiresome circle dance.

So, who do you think had the most credibility with me—Jack or Alice? Surely, that's an easy question to answer—a setup, really. Of course, it's Jack, but why? Because Jack did what he said he would do. Alice did not. At the end of the day, it is right actions, not good intentions, that make the difference. And here is why this is so important. If we desire to exercise fidelity to every trust, we must first have the credibility to be entrusted. If not, we are simply untrustworthy, and no one will place their trust in us, nor should they. So, the way to begin the practice of exercising fidelity to every trust is to examine honestly your own credibility—to do a credibility check. Can others truly count on me? As with many virtues, we often hold others to a much higher standard than we do ourselves. So, start with a ruthless self-credibility check. And ask an honest and trusted friend, too. As with most spiritual practices, interior work comes first.

Fidelity

Fidelity can be understood in several different, but related ways: as a strict observance of promises, as loyalty to friends, and as a careful adherence to fact and detail. Each understanding is important as we work to exercise fidelity carefully and consistently in our daily lives.

Promises

The first meaning makes it clear that keeping your promises is at the heart of fidelity. My parents would tell me, "Your word is your bond. Say what you mean, and do what you say." Honestly, I didn't understand the full implications of what a bond was, but I did understand that your word was to mean something. You were to keep your promises. And I understood even then that if you didn't keep your promises, you lost something very dear to you—your credibility and your integrity.

There are three rather simple but profound ways to keep your promises. The first is this: don't make promises you can't keep. I learned this the hard way rather early in my work as an academic dean, while working with faculty and professional staff. Someone would come to my office, wanting me to support an idea or pay for some trip. I would say, "Of course," wanting to be liked and appreciated. However, sometimes I would make promises that were not mine to make. My boss would rightfully disagree or I had no budget to cover the expenses, so I would have to go back and say, "Sorry, I tried but I could not make it happen." Along with eating a little crow, I lost some credibility. I soon learned that it was much better to say, "I like the idea, so if I can say yes I will, but this is not my sole decision to make. Let me do my best and get back to you." In those instances when I came back with a "no," I won respect for trying rather than losing credibility by making a promise that I could not keep.

A second way to be sure to keep your promises is this: don't make promises you don't intend to keep. Now, I know that this is self-evident, but to be honest, we all do it sometimes. I know I do. We don't want to hurt someone's feelings or decline when we are put on the spot to agree, going along with a dinner invitation or a committee decision when you know deep down that you will later change your tune. It can easily happen when someone invites you for dinner. You say, "Okay, that would be great!" However, the truth is that you have no intention of going to dinner with this person. You simply opt for the easy way out. You know full well that you will call back or send an email later begging off due to a calendar conflict. At the moment, these actions are more comfortable and less embarrassing, but in the long run, there is integrity to be lost, too. And I know that speaking in opposition at a meeting can be daunting, but trying to backtrack because you didn't speak your mind and honestly express your reservations has its own set of difficulties, too. Many times in meetings and conversations like this, others are thinking or feeling the same way. When you express your reservations, it gives others a chance to speak out, too. In doing so, poor decisions can often be modified or avoided altogether. So, even when it is tricky or painful or embarrassing, don't make promises you have no intention of keeping.

Finally, if you desire to exercise a strict observance of promises, it means that you have to keep the promises that you make, too. For many of us, this is the most frequent and difficult aspect of promise-keeping. What do you do when you are offered tickets to the big football game on the same day when you said that you would help out with dinner and cleanup at the homeless shelter? What happens when you receive a better offer on the car you are selling, just after you verbally agreed to another offer? What happens when you are invited to the university president's home for a special dinner, but you are already committed to dinner that same night with a new couple from church? And what happens when you receive a new job offer with a 20 percent increase in salary, just a week after you signed and returned your annual contract to your present employer? These are difficult, of course, but I am suggesting that we hold ourselves to a higher standard than the law. If you want your word to be your bond, then it has to mean something—even if it involves a loss in income or a chance to do something really special. In God's economy, it is the deal with the highest integrity rather than the deal with the highest returns that is the best course of action. Be known for keeping the promises that you make. At times, you may forfeit some immediate gains, but you'll sleep better with your integrity in tact. It is one of the keys to living a simple, sincere, and serene life.

Loyalty

The second meaning of fidelity is loyalty, especially to your friends. Let's face it, maintaining strong and vibrant friendships can sometimes be challenging, particularly so when your friends are not perfect. Of course, they have flaws and idiosyncrasies, and they come up short from time to time much like we do, but we are so much more understanding and forgiving of our own actions, aren't we? A real act of fidelity is to be loyal to your friends despite their flaws and, in fact, in full recognition of them. It is a loyal friend who knows you and sees you for who you are, and walks with you anyway.

Another aspect of loyalty is to be dependable, to be a person that your friends can count on to do what you say—every time. And when help is needed, you show up. Loyalty also implies an unswerving, steadfast commitment. One who can be counted on for the long haul, not just when things are going smoothly. Anyone who has been fired or removed from a prominent position or suffered a public failure can testify to the reality of this statement: In hard times, you can tell who your true friends really are—and there aren't many. This is sad, but true. In hard and difficult times, it is easy to become virtually invisible. It is your loyal friends who show up and walk with you. They look in your eyes as if to say, "I see you," proffering one of the most precious gifts that loyalty can bestow. It is terrible to feel invisible—at work, in church, or just about anywhere else for that matter.

Of course, being loyal does not require your friends to approve of all the things you do. Rather, a loyal friend stands by you and with you in spite of your actions, but they will also speak truthfully and hold you accountable. In these instances, loyalty is grace in action, but it is grace with eyes wide open—no heads buried in the sand.

Adherence to Fact or Detail

A third aspect of fidelity means a steadfast allegiance to the truth, a commitment to accuracy, honestly, and truth-telling. It is akin to the oath we take in court: to tell the truth (honesty), the whole truth (being forthcoming and candid), and nothing but the truth (accuracy). Of course, it is important to be honest, and also to be sensitive to the feelings of others. Even if you don't like the dress someone is wearing, you are under no obligation to walk over to that person and state your opinion. Some things are better kept to yourself (including most of your fashion opinions). This is not what telling the whole truth means. Here we are talking about not withholding pertinent information or details to permit or encourage someone to come to an erroneous opinion or finding. In this case, telling a half-truth is a form of deception.

Of course, telling a "one and a half-truth" is a form of deception, too. The common word for this behavior is exaggeration, embellishing the facts to make a better description of events or to look better than the facts honestly allow. When we are found out, we lose trust. At this point, however, I want to be sure to make an important distinction. Many of us are known to be "storytellers"—I know I am. And I am asked from time to time, "Is that story you just told true? Did it really happen?" Sometimes I give the answer I heard once from a Native American wisdom keeper here in the Northwest. He said, "I am going to tell you a story. It is a true story. It didn't really happen, but it is nonetheless a true story." From this it is easy to see that stories can contain compelling truths, even if the facts are fictional or embellished in some way. There is nothing untrustworthy about that. In fact, Jesus taught in parables. These stories conveyed deep truths, but they didn't necessarily happen. They were stories with a real message.

The trouble comes when stories are presented as factual when they are not. When we tell stories and invent facts and events, particularly the facts and events of our own lives, to make us seem more accomplished or adventurous than we actually are, we become storytellers of a different kind. We cross the integrity line and try to sell fiction as fact. When we are found out, others have little reason to trust what we have to say about anything, even when what we have to say is true. We become untrustworthy, and with good reason.

At the end of the day, the three aspects of fidelity go hand in hand. Consistently keeping your promises, being loyal to your friends, and conscientiously telling the truth engender credibility, and as we have noted earlier in this chapter, credibility is a key to being trustworthy. Exercising fidelity to every trust requires credibility to be sure, but trust in what? Are we talking about something that has been entrusted to us, or something in us? And what does it mean to have fidelity in *every* trust? These questions will be explored in the following section.

Trust

When we pray and work to exercise "fidelity to every trust" as a spiritual practice, there are two dimensions of trust to take into account. The first is entrustment, to be entrusted. That is, we have something to care for or keep safe. When my best friend in grade school went off to summer camp for two weeks, he entrusted his baseball glove to me. It was a solemn obligation that I took seriously. I was to look after it, and return it to him in good condition. As I look back, he probably thought it was better to entrust his glove to my care rather than to hide it in his room, hoping that his younger brothers would not find it and use it as a makeshift kickball. In any case, I was entrusted with the glove, and I cared for it faithfully.

We can all think of times that we have been entrusted to care for something that was precious to someone else—a house, a car, or a pet. Of course, there are other things, perhaps more important things, that require our care, too. The first is a confidence. When someone takes us into his or her confidence, she is entrusting us with something extremely valuable. This is no small or menial task. However, there is something in the human spirit that pulls us to share what we know, to be the one with some hot news. Why is it so intriguing and exciting to say, "Now don't tell anyone else, but did you know . . .?" Keeping a confidence is one of the truest tests of our integrity, and I know I fail that test more often than I would like to admit. I have learned, though, that when I watchfully remind myself that to care for a confidence is far more important than to care for a neighbor's pet, it puts it into perspective for me. If I don't take care of the confidences that are entrusted to me, I am simply not worthy of their trust. Being trustworthy is a choice.

I have come to believe that we have also been entrusted with our neighbors. The Scriptures tell us to love them as we love ourselves (Lev 19:18), and Jesus affirmed the importance of doing so many times (Matt 22:39; Mark 12:31; Luke 10:28). I try to walk in my neighborhood regularly, and when I do, I reflect on the fact that in some deep way, it is in my care.

That is, I am to care for my neighbors. And as I walk, I pray for discernment and insight, for eyes to see and ears to hear how I can express care, compassion, connection, and love to those who have pitched their tents near mine.

And I believe that the entire creation has been entrusted to us, too. I used to think that all of creation was given to us for our personal use. We could do with it as we wished. However, I think the idea of entrustment rather than possession is a better way to think about this relationship. I didn't own my best friend's baseball glove; it was entrusted to me. I was to care for it and return it in good shape. I think about the earth in a similar way. We don't own it, but it is under our care. Whenever I see the elderly out planting trees in the public park, I am deeply moved. It is obvious that they are planting trees for someone else. They will never enjoy the shade of these trees when they are full-grown, but they plant nonetheless, investing in the future. I think that that is a good way to approach all of creation. We are entrusted not only with the present, but with the future, even if we won't fully share in it.

In addition to thinking of trust as entrustment, we can also think about trust in terms of what we "trust in." That is to say, we not only "care for" things that are entrusted to us, but we place our trust in other things, too. If we pray for help in exercising fidelity to every trust, does that mean we are to be faithful to the things we put our trust in, too? The short answer is yes. A longer answer starts with the acknowledgement that we put our trust in things all the time, and the manner and extent to which we do shapes us deeply. Let's look at three aspects of "trusting in." As it turns out, "trusting in" is a spiritual practice.

First, we place our trust in others. Actually, we do this every time we drive a car over a bridge or make a left turn in heavy traffic, fly in a plane, follow directions, eat some ice cream, or buy online. We have to trust systems, organizations, neighbors, and strangers all the time. But trust comes hard for many of us. Why? Honestly, some of us seem to have a more optimistic spirit about others, partly because of the way we were brought up to see the world, and partly because if you live long enough, someone is going to disappoint you and let you down. Certainly, the track record isn't perfect, but it is helpful to note that ours isn't either. I have come to believe that trusting in others will lead to disappointment at times, but crafting a life without trust is fearful, isolating, and spiritually harmful. It robs us of much community, connection, and joy.

Second, we place trust in ourselves. As with trust in others, some of us are better at it than others, and better at it at some times than at others. I get that. And of course, there are those who have such an inflated opinion of themselves that they are difficult, even painful, to be around. They place all their trust in themselves. I get that, too, but I still argue that it is important to have a deep sense of faith in who you are, simply trusting in your own talents, passions, dreams, opportunities, and future—things that have been entrusted to you. Such trust is a spiritual practice, and it will shape you in positive ways.

And finally, we all place our trust in God, to some extent or another. And the extent to which we do shapes our abilities to trust in others and in ourselves, too. For me, there is great comfort in seeing life as a journey, knowing that I can trust in God's grace, God's presence, and God's timing. I have come to believe that life has seasons. In some seasons, it is difficult to understand why we can't find a job, or why things are going so poorly at work or at the church, but it is comforting to know that seasons do pass. It isn't permanent—after winter comes spring. Trusting in God means trusting that things are happening, even when it seems that nothing in happening. And placing our trust in God not only for the present, but for the future, too, brings a sense of rootedness and security that few of your friends will understand. Even when the answer to our prayers seems to be "no" or "not now," or they are met with silence, our trust in God grounds us with an underlying confidence that is comforting to have and beautiful to behold.

I worry that all this talk about trust may sound a bit too simplistic, even naïve. Maybe it is, but honestly I don't think so. I know that life is terribly complicated and some of us face realities and difficulties beyond imagination, but at the same time, I do not want to underemphasize the spiritual importance of having a healthy trust—trust in others, trust in ourselves, and trust in God. It is a spiritual discipline, something you commit to undertake with God's help. And the spiritual practice of exercising fidelity to *every* trust, not just the ones that are convenient or immediately helpful, will shape you deeply. Even in difficult climates and hostile soil, it is a plant worth nourishing, and its fruit will sustain you in the most difficult of times.

Scripture

Before we end this chapter with some practical words of advice, I want to examine three Old Testament passages that illustrate fidelity to every trust. Two are affirming and positive; the other not so much. We'll start with the story of King Hezekiah, found in Isaiah. During the time when kings ruled Israel and Judah, God spoke through prophets. Their primary role was to call God's people back to him. Sometimes they spoke directly to the king. In this particular case, the prophet, Isaiah, went to King Hezekiah and said, "Hear the word of the Lord Almighty: The time will surely come when everything in your palace, and all that your predecessors have stored up until this day, will be carried off to Babylon. Nothing will be left, says the Lord" (Isa 39:5–6). What devastating news—all your possessions will be lost—but Isaiah wasn't finished. He adds, "And some of your descendants, your own flesh and blood who will be born to you, will be taken away, and they will become eunuchs in the palace of the king of Babylon" (Isa 39:7). Even more devastating, your own family will be taken into captivity as slaves to another king. Terrible news! And how did the king respond to this prophecy from Isaiah? "The word of the Lord is good," Hezekiah replied. For he thought, "There will be peace and security in my lifetime" (Isa 39: 8). Good news? Really? Your family will be taken into slavery and that is *good* news? Yes, it was good news to Hezekiah because he was only interested in himself, in the present. He recognized neither obligation nor concern for his family or for the future. Whew, all is good because it will be good for *me*! This is not an example of exercising fidelity to every trust.

Fortunately, there are many examples of trust-keeping in Scripture as well. I think of Ruth and her mother-in-law, Naomi, recorded in the book of Ruth. Naomi's husband died, and later her two sons died, too. Naomi and her two daughters-in-law were left to fend for themselves in the full force of a widespread famine. Naomi insisted that her daughters-in-law leave her and return to their own people and their own gods. One daughter-in-law, Orpah, did, but Ruth would not go. She wouldn't leave her mother-in-law alone, saying, "Don't urge me to leave you or to turn back from you. Where you go I will go, and where you stay I will stay. Your people will be my people and your God my God. Where you die I will die, and there I will be buried" (Ruth 1:16–17). What an incredible example of loyalty, of being faithful to every trust. And while the story has a very happy ending, I think it would be a marvelous story of faithfulness to every trust, regardless of the rest of the story.

And finally, there is Nathan, a prophet who at incredible personal risk confronted King David about having Beersheba's husband killed in battle so he could marry her himself. (See 2 Samuel 12 for the complete story.) Fortunately for Nathan, King David was receptive to his prophetic rebuke, repenting for what he had done instead of killing the messenger. It took great courage for Nathan to call the king to accountability, but he was faithful to his calling. It is little wonder that when King David desperately needed someone he could trust to accompany his son, Solomon, to the place where he would be anointed king, he sent for Nathan. Nathan, you see, was trustworthy, faithful to every trust. He would keep his promises, even at the risk of his own life.

Some Practical Advice

As you pray to exercise fidelity to every trust, here are several practical ways to begin this effort. Take a TRIP (trust retreat for insight and prayer). Set aside a half-day to be alone, providing a block of uninterrupted time for candid introspection without distractions. First, focus your thoughts and prayers on promises. What promises have I made? Make a list. Honestly, do I keep them? Do any shortcomings come to mind? Put them on the list, too. Is there any way to go back and honor those commitments now? If so, how would you do it, and if not, is at least an apology or some other act of reconciliation in order?

Do a loyalty check. Who are the friends who have stood by you, who you can always count on? Make a list, and find a time in the next week to tell them so. Are there friends or family who are in need or hurting right now? If so, what can you do to stand by them and communicate, "I see you." And do you know of anyone who is without friends, lonely souls who are making their way solo? Think about how you could be a friend to them.

Conclude your TRIP by prayerfully asking this question: Do I tell the truth? Be open to the prompting of the Holy Spirit. As things come to mind, write them down, too, and resolve with God's help to practice truthfulness. When you return from your TRIP, you will have a good list to review daily as you pray, "help me to exercise fidelity to every trust." And as you do, you will see your spiritual garden grow.

Another practical word of advice may sound simple, but it is really a rigorous spiritual discipline: look for the good in others, and see the good in all things. This is really difficult, but with practice you will get better at it. I have come to believe that we usually see what we are looking for. If we look for flaws, we will see them. Instead, I choose to see the strengths in others rather than their faults. It's my choice really. And if we look through the eyes of our souls, I believe that we will begin to see good in all things. It is not that all things are good, but rather that our loving God is always with us, working to redeem even our worst mistakes and failures. God is good all the time, and there is nothing we can do to make God stop loving us. We can see good in all things just as God sees good things in all of us.

Conclusion

In this chapter, we began by looking at credibility—we have to be trustworthy—and examined three aspects of fidelity: promises (don't make promises you can't keep, don't make promises you don't intend to keep, and keep the promises you make); loyalty (be loyal and steadfast, not because your friends are perfect, but in full recognition that we are all broken, be loyal anyway); and truth-telling (carefully adhering to fact and detail, not telling more than you should or more than you know). We looked next at two elements of trust: trust of (things we have been given to care for—relationships, obligations, neighbors, the earth) and trust in (in others, in ourselves, and in God). Three examples from Scripture were noted that describe different aspects of fidelity to every trust: King Hezekiah (a poor example of entrustment), Ruth and Naomi (loyalty), and the prophet Nathan and King David (faithfulness to calling and earned credibility). We ended with two practical ways to get started with the spiritual practice of exercising faithfulness to every trust (take a TRIP—a trust retreat for insight and prayer, and determine to look for the good in others and see the good in all things).

At the end of the day, I realize how difficult it is to be faithful to every trust (or any spiritual practice, for that matter), and I recognize that without God's help, we won't see much growth in our spiritual garden. The good news is that God is eager to partner with us. That is why we pray "A Morning Resolve" rather than just resolve to do all of this on our own. Our spiritual formation begins when we place our trust in God. David wrote in Psalm 34:8, "Taste and see that the Lord is good." That's good advice. Taste away!

Questions for Discussion and Reflection

1. Why do you think it is so hard for so many of us to keep a confidence?

2. What aspect of trusting is most difficult for you—trusting in others, trusting in yourself, or trusting in God and God's timing? Why?

3. Think of someone who has become invisible or is now off the radar in your church or community. What could you do to reach out and make contact?

4. As a steward of your neighborhood, what could you do to demonstrate your care and concern?

5. If we take the proposition seriously that the future is entrusted to us as well as the present, what would that mean for you? What could you do now to care for the future?

I will try this day to live a simple, sincere, and serene life, repelling promptly every thought of discontent, anxiety, discouragement, impurity, and self-seeking; cultivating cheerfulness, magnanimity, charity, and the habit of holy silence; exercising economy in expenditure, generosity in giving, carefulness in conversation, diligence in appointed service, fidelity to every trust . . .

— 13 —

A Childlike Faith in God

There are only two ways to live ... one is as though nothing is a miracle ... the other is as if everything is.

—*ALBERT EINSTEIN*

Introduction

I HAVE TO ADMIT that I like signs, and I look for them all the time. Notice that I didn't say that I look at them, but I look for them. Sometimes, I actually think they look for me, too. Obviously, I am not talking about commercial advertising along the side of the freeway. Rather, I am talking about spiritual signs, events, and occasions that speak to me in deep (and I would add mysterious) ways. Some signs are quite familiar to many of us. Take the rainbow, for example. Some view it as a reminder of a promise that we will not see another massive flood, necessitating the building of an ark. Others see it as a marker for a hidden pot of gold. Most of us are taken by its sheer beauty and wonder. While science describes a rainbow as an optical illusion, the result of the reflection, refraction, and dispersion of light in water droplets, I must admit that I see a miracle, finding joy and taking comfort every time I see one. It never gets old. I join Einstein in seeing another dimension, a miracle that is difficult to explain but real nonetheless.

Let me tell you about two of my favorite signs. While I was walking along Hapuna Beach on the Big Island of Hawaii, two humpback whales breached the water side by side less than fifty yards from shore. I was deeply moved. Without thinking, I exclaimed, "It's a sign from God!" When I returned to the university, I told a colleague about what I saw and what I said. Her response was, "A sign from God? What did it mean?" When I told her that I really didn't know, she shook for her head and walked away. Apparently, if you don't know what it means, it doesn't count.

The second sign has to do with mushrooms. As a boy, my dad and I would head to the woods in the spring to look for mushrooms, morel mushrooms to be precise. To me, they were simply the best. What a joy it was to find a small patch and bring them home for dinner. Over the years, on three separate occasions when I was truly concerned about an uncertain future, I walked into a patch of morels. The first time, I was leaving a farm in Tennessee that I very much loved, so I decided to take just one more walk around the property. It was a very sad day. Just across the creek, I ducked into a small grove of trees and there they were, an entire patch of morels. I took it as a sign.

The second time, I was selling a new house and leaving my job in Indiana, heading for California. I was worried about the transition and the uncertain financial and social details of leaving the Midwest and settling in Southern California on short notice. On the day before the movers were to arrive, I read in the local newspaper that it was mushroom season, so on a whim I walked across the street and down a wooded hillside. What did I find but a nice patch of morels! I had them for lunch, and took it as a sign.

Three years later, I was at low tide in my personal life—deeply discouraged and feeling very much alone. As I left my office in San Diego that evening, I walked up the sidewalk by the church across the way. The week before, their flower beds received a fresh layer of mulch. As I made my way, I suddenly stopped and stared. I couldn't believe my eyes. There, in the middle of the flower bed, was a beautiful morel mushroom, a big one. I was so surprised because you don't find many morels growing along the California coast, but there it was. I brought it home, fixed it for dinner, and took it as a sign, too.

So, were these signs? I say yes. Were they signs from God? I can't say, but I think so. Could they be just a series of coincidences? Of course, but I can tell you this, the whales and the mushrooms spoke to my spirit and brought comfort. That is enough for me. I need no other explanation. If this is an expression of a childlike faith, then I need more of it.

As we get older, why does everything have to have a logical explanation—or it doesn't count? What is it about adulthood that negates much of the wonder and mystery in our daily lives—and in our faith? How can we pray to exercise a childlike faith in God without being childish? Is it possible to exercise a simple faith without being silly or stupid? I honestly believe that we can. This is the heart of this chapter, exploring first what it means to have a childlike faith, and then what it means to place our faith in God. As you will see, it has a great deal to do with trust.

A Childlike Faith

On one occasion while Jesus was teaching, his disciples tried to keep the little children away. After all, Jesus was busy bringing in the kingdom, surely an adult thing. Jesus was quite indignant. He wanted the little children to be present, and he said that we would all do well to have a childlike faith, too (Matt 19:13-15; Mark 10:13-16; Luke 18:15-17). So, what is a childlike faith, and how is it different from an adult faith? Aren't we to grow and mature in our faith? The answer to this last question is yes; we are to grow and mature in our faith. We are to put away childish things, but clearly Jesus saw something very important in the faith of a child that he commended to all of us. What are those aspects of a childlike faith that are important for us to retain and practice? Here, we will look briefly at four that we can rediscover or recover and put into practice: curiosity, imagination, wonder, and trust.

Curiosity

I know that children can drive you almost crazy with their two fundamental questions: "What is that?" and "Why?" As children start to acquire recognition and language skills, we point to a picture of a cow and ask, "What is that?" They say, "cow" and we clap our hands in celebration. And as we read to them, we point to all the animals, trees, vehicles, and colors in the book and ask the same question, "What is that?" All well and good, but there comes a day when the roles are reversed. The child walks around all day asking you, "What is this, what is that, what are you doing, or where are you going?" Honestly, it can be overwhelming at times, but a natural curiosity is a wonderful thing to behold. Sadly, it is somehow schooled out of us by the time we reach adulthood. How many of us have said to a child, "You ask too many questions"? As we become grown-ups, most of us learn to hold our curiosities in check and stop asking so many questions. When we do, we lose something quite extraordinary, and particularly so if we stop asking questions about our faith, about God. As we become preoccupied with having the right answers rather than asking good questions, we can lose our way. In our spiritual gardens, we want to cultivate living, organic, fruit-bearing plants, not install stone monuments dedicated to the truth as we see it. I have come to believe that curiosity is an almost forgotten spiritual practice, and that God loves to hear our questions. Maturity comes when we can have a long list of questions, but we are comfortable with not having or needing all the answers. It is a simple and sincere practice, but not a silly one.

Imagination

When my parents went to visit my second-grade class on Parents Night, they noticed that the teacher had posted on the walls some of the things her students had shared during show-and-tell time. What caught their interest was a particular sign that read, "Patrick had a bat fly through his living room last week!" Imagine their astonishment, since to their recollection, no such event ever happened. Under questioning, I had to admit that I made it up and shared it with the class because I forgot to bring something of interest to share that day. However, I was quick to add that I had imagined that such an event could happen. My mother told me that an active imagination is a good thing, but it is always important to keep a clear distinction between fact and fiction, and not peddle one for the other. Now, clearly this is not the kind of imagination that builds spiritual character, but there is an aspect of imagination that does. Let me explain.

I think the key idea is to retain an active imagination, something that seems to get schooled out of us along with curiosity as we mature. Sadly, this can be so limiting for our spiritual growth. When I watch children at play, their imaginations are in full gear. I smile when I hear their conversations about dragons, gigantic flying birds, superheroes, games, rules, and championships. There is certainly more going on in the room than meets the eye. When we lose the ability to imagine, our play and our worship are diminished, often becoming sober and ceremonial activities. Being somber is not a spiritual practice that takes much effort.

However, seeing possibilities in our own circumstances and in the lives of others that are not evident at the time are acts of faith, a childlike faith. It can be recovered with intention and practice. A good place to start is to spend more time playing with kids. They will teach you a great deal about life, and about using your imagination, too. The joy that comes from a childlike imagination and play contributes so much to a simple, sincere, and serene life.

Wonder

What comes to mind when you think of the word *wonder*? For me, it is amazement, astonishment, surprise, and awe. These are good words, child-like attributes. What would it mean for you to rediscover and intentionally practice wonder in your spiritual life, as an act of worship or a spiritual discipline? To be aware that in the middle of your daily, not-so-marvelous life you can be surprised and amazed beyond imagination is the place to start, and when you intentionally look for such events, occasions, and settings as you pray for help in exercising a childlike faith in God, I truly believe that you will discover a spiritual reality beyond imagination. When you look around with a childlike spiritual lens, you will find yourself saying "wow" more often than not. It is a holy wow, to be sure, just like the first time you look over the rim of the Grand Canyon. It simply exceeds anything you could describe and imagine. Most of us, after attempting to take a few photos of the canyon, or the redwoods, or the ocean, simply stop taking pictures and look around with a deep sense of wonder. Pictures just can't capture what we are seeing and feeling. With practice, I believe that our spiritual lens can provide for us the same delight right in our own neighborhoods. Most things in life don't live up to their hype, but God's grace isn't on that list. Neither is a childlike faith.

Trust

Children surely ask a lot of questions, but they also display a deep element of trust, too. If you say to most kids, "Come on, hop in the car, let's go," they will ask, "Where are we going?"—even as they are getting in the car. I think that is one of the keys to a childlike faith. They are curious, to be sure, but they get in the car with their questions unanswered. There is an underlying faith and trust in the adult. The eleventh chapter of Hebrews is often referred to as the faith chapter. One of my favorite verses in the entire Bible is this: "By faith Abraham, when called to go to a place he would later receive as his inheritance, obeyed and went, even though he did not know where he was going" (Heb 11:8). Abraham heard the call, obeyed, and went.

125

Oh, I'm sure he had a question or two about the entire affair, and you know his family certainly did, but even while the questions were flying, they were on the journey and making their way. That's childlike faith in action, and it is neither childish nor silly. For most of us, however, as we mature, skepticism, sarcasm, and cynicism begin to creep in. They infect a spiritual garden like bad weeds. The challenge, it seems to me, is to live with a profound spiritual sense of trust, in spite of so many messages to the contrary. Put another way, we don't deny the darkness but we choose not to live in it, knowing that with just a little bit of light, we can make our way through the night. The key is to place our trust in the right things, or in this case, in the right person, in someone who's character deserves our trust: God.

Faith in God

I want to be clear that to exercise a childlike faith can be silly, even dangerous, if it is misplaced. In "A Morning Resolve," we are not simply praying to develop a childlike faith, but rather a childlike faith *in God*. To place our confidence in others, in our successes, our families, our possessions, or our jobs is to invite disillusionment and tragedy. No, we pray for a childlike faith in God, in his goodness, his grace, his presence, his everlasting love, and his leading in our lives. That anchors our faith in something very real. Ultimately, it is God's dependable character that allows us to follow like a child, to obey and go, even when we do not know where we are going. In the next section, we will look at two scriptural passages, the first providing some insight into a childlike faith, and the second, some insight into what happens when suspicion and distrust creep in.

Scripture

In an earlier chapter, we briefly visited the story of the High Priest, Eli, and the young boy, Samuel, who had been entrusted to his care and tutelage. As 1 Samuel tells us, "In those days, the word of the Lord was rare; there were not many visions" (3:1), yet the Lord came and spoke to Samuel one night. Obviously, Samuel was unfamiliar with God's voice, having not personally heard it before or even heard adults speaking much about such matters. Understandably, he thought that Eli was calling, so he went immediately to him. Eli, half asleep, sent him back to bed, not once, but twice! On the third time, though, Eli figured it out. He told Samuel that it was the Lord who was calling, and if he spoke again to simply say, "Speak for your servant is listening" (1 Sam 3:10). Samuel listened, and God gave him a message for Eli—and not a happy one at that. But when Eli pressed him for the message from God, he delivered that, too.

There are several things I want to point out here. First, Samuel was unfamiliar with God's voice, so he ran to Eli's side. Still today, hearing God's voice can be confusing, especially in a culture with so much noise and distraction. Young people need to have wise friends around who can help interpret the messages they hear. When they do hear God speaking, it is important to have someone close by, someone they trust, who can interpret for them. This is one reason why intergenerational relationships are so important. Second, when Eli told Samuel how to answer the Lord, he simply followed instructions, exercising a childlike faith in Eli. However, in the end, he displayed a childlike faith in God by sharing God's message for Eli in no uncertain terms. That was a bit risky. Eli could have chosen to shoot the messenger, or summarily dismiss him along with the message. He did not, and the rest is history. Samuel became a transitional leader between the time of the judges and the reigns of the kings. In fact, he appointed Israel's first king. A childlike faith took root in the heart of a great servant.

The second passage provides an example of how distrust and suspicion can creep in and compromise a childlike faith, even in the best of leaders. Here I am thinking of Joshua, just before he fought the battle of Jericho. When Moses died, Joshua became the leader of God's people, overseeing the crossing of the Jordan River and pressing the battle for Jericho and the surrounding territory. On the road near Jericho, Joshua looked up and saw a man standing in front of him. "Are you for us or for our enemies?" Joshua asked (Josh 5:13). Of course, in a battle zone, this is a fair question, because the world is split up into two sides—our side and the other side. Interestingly, the person (who turned out to be a messenger from the Lord) responded, "Neither" (Josh 5:14). Even in the midst of battle and hostility, this was not about taking sides—or seeing sides. I worry about a world view that sees friends and enemies, good and evil, them and us. To me, it is not the most helpful approach for exercising a childlike faith in God, at times inviting too much mistrust and fear into our lives. Is there a more helpful way to relate to those we do not know, or to new situations? The key, I believe, is to be as wise as serpents and as gentle as doves. That is to say, a childlike faith in God does not mean that we unplug our brains or put our children in harm's way. Rather, it is the combination of wisdom and gentleness that leads to a simple, sincere, and serene life. Of course, this takes practice, but an underlying faith in God's goodness and constant presence provides a solid footing from which to proceed.

Some Practical Advice

When my mother started driving a big yellow school bus, I would sometimes get the opportunity to ride with her as she made her kindergarten run at noon. On the way to the elementary school, we had to cross a railroad track. Every time, she would stop the bus, purposefully look both ways, open the door, and listen before proceeding. At the time, stopping an empty school bus seemed silly to me, but now that I look back and see the wisdom in the routine. Sadly, it is easy to miss something even as large and noisy as an oncoming train if you're not paying attention. If this is the case, how much easier is it to miss God's still small voice and direction in our lives. Sometimes I wish God would be more pushy, but he seems to bide his time and wait patiently. So, my four words of practical advice for exercising a childlike faith in God are: stop, look, listen, and ask.

First, slow down and stop for a bit. We live at such a frenetic pace that we don't even see the railroad crossings, let alone hear the trains. Take an hour and think about your schedule. For many of us, it will be hard to find even an hour to do so, but if we are truly interested in cultivating a simple, sincere, and serene life, we have to make conscious and consistent spaces in our daily lives for an encounter with God; to recognize that each day is an encounter with God. The first step is not really a step at all, but rather a decision to stop walking and be still.

Then, look for signs all around you, and don't try to figure them out. You don't have to know what they all mean—they still count. Part of the mystery and magnificence is that there is a spiritual dimension to all of life, even in our most mundane activities like going to the grocery store or mowing the grass. While we all have "thin places" in our lives like the ocean or the redwoods where heaven and earth seem to intersect and we feel especially close to God, I believe that thin places are all over the place—especially in our own neighborhoods. The key, it seems to me, is to be mindful; if we want to find them, we have to stop and look with spiritual intent. God can speak to you in ways that you can't explain—and you don't need to.

The third instruction is to listen. Are there times in your day when you can really be present to listen to others, or when God can speak to you?

So much of our prayer life (such as it is) is given over to requests, explanations, concerns—all ours. We do all the talking. When is it that you say, "Speak, Lord, for your servant is listening?" And then actually take the time to listen. The Quakers believe that God is speaking to everyone all the time. It is our job to learn to recognize the voice, stop, listen, and then follow. That's good advice for all of us.

So, much like the rules for safe school bus driving, our job is to stop, look, and listen. I would add one more: question. I have come to believe that the process of asking the right questions is far more important than trying to come up with a long list of the right answers, and then demanding that everyone conform to them or they don't belong. It is easy to confuse rational knowledge with wisdom. In my experience, the truly wise among us are much more comfortable with ambiguity, with not having all the answers. They use words like "I don't know, I'm not sure, what do you think, wow," and "could be" rather than "here's the right (and only) answer; I know—you follow." Asking questions promotes a deep and lasting dialogue, particularly so if value is placed as much on the process as on the results. I have come to believe that asking earnest questions and listening to each other is one of the purest forms of hospitality, a spiritual discipline, and it is best served with a generous portion of humility.

Conclusion

In this chapter, we examined what it means to exercise a childlike faith in God, noting that a childlike faith isn't childish or silly at all. It involves curiosity, imagination, wonder, and trust—attributes that children are better at than most adults. And we noted the importance of having a childlike faith in God, not just a conjectural faith in "whatever." We can place our trust in God's love, God's presence, God's promises, and God's character, providing an anchor for our faith. We looked at the story of Samuel and Eli to see a childlike faith in action, and we saw how fear and mistrust can color our view of the world in the story of such a great figure as Joshua. Finally, four words of practical advice were offered: stop, look, listen, and question. These are, it turns out, serious spiritual practices, and they will bear good fruit.

Questions for Discussion and Reflection

1. Of the four attributes of a childlike faith—curiosity, imagination, wonder, and trust—which comes easiest for you? Which is the most difficult? Why?

2. Why do you think it is so difficult in our society to trust anything? Is it naïve to think we can trust others? Trust God?

3. Can you think of a time when you helped someone else recognize God's voice? Has anyone ever done that for you? What was the result?

4. Have you seen any signs lately? How is God speaking to you? Are you actively listening for his voice?

5. Think of a time when you heard God's voice and, like Abraham, you went, even though you didn't know where you were going. What happened? Would you do it again? What do you think is the biggest impediment from doing what God calls us to do?

I will try this day to live a simple, sincere, and serene life, repelling promptly every thought of discontent, anxiety, discouragement, impurity, and self-seeking; cultivating cheerfulness, magnanimity, charity, and the habit of holy silence; exercising economy in expenditure, generosity in giving, carefulness in conversation, diligence in appointed service, fidelity to every trust, and a childlike faith in God . . .

* * *

French Fries of Grace—A Story

In my hometown, Bernie Smith was a rich man—or at least, we thought so. Not only did he own the A&P grocery store, he also owned a small restaurant across the street—one with a neon sign in front that blinked EAT in big orange letters. The chairs in the restaurant were covered with a bright red plastic, and there were four white plastic-covered stools at the counter.

Bernie Smith was not only the owner; he was also the fry cook. We admired a person who could hold down two jobs at the same time.

Sometimes my grandfather would take some of the Allen boys to Bernie's, and we would sit at the counter and voraciously consume a hamburger and chocolate malt. All of a sudden, Bernie Smith would throw a frozen French fry from the kitchen and hit one of us right in the forehead. What an honor it was to be the one singled out for such attention.

My mother shopped at the A&P every Saturday morning, and once each month it was my turn to go with her. My three brothers had to stay home with Dad, so it was a real treat to be with Mom and have her undivided attention. If we didn't need to purchase a large sack of flour, I would ride on the bottom rack of the grocery cart. Sometimes I would reach out from under the cart and grab someone's ankle in passing. I thought it was kind of funny to hear a middle-aged person yell in that sleepy little grocery store. However, mother didn't seem to see the humor in such events, so I agreed under threat of severe punishment that I would refrain from any further such activities. It was probably a very wise decision.

One day while the cart was in the checkout line, I looked over from my favorite riding position under the cart and saw a big box of Black Jack gum on the bottom shelf. Given cover by the groceries in the cart, I reached out, took a pack of gum, and stuffed it in my pocket. On the way home, I opened the pack and started to chew. My mother noticed what I was doing and without saying a word, pulled the car over to the side of the road and turned off the engine. I was busted and I knew it. She told me that I had just committed a Class B felony in the state of Michigan. She also told me that I would be summarily punished and then uttered those seven words that every child fears most: just wait until your dad gets home.

I was on my best behavior the rest of the day—giving compliments to Mom about her hair (that wasn't easy), offering to set the table for dinner, and being as nice as humanly possible to my younger brothers. I even asked to be excused from the table and raced off to my room without dessert. Of course, in the end, it didn't help. After dinner, Dad came to my room and made me cry by saying that he was disappointed in me. Then, he made me cry by administering corporal punishment. He said it hurt him more than it hurt me, but I failed to follow the logic. Anyway, I took my lumps and was ready to move on—but then the other shoe dropped!

I was informed that I would have to go back to the store, tell Bernie Smith what I had done, say that I was sorry, and pay for the gum with my own money. I asked for another spanking instead. It proved to be the hardest thing I had ever done. Even though Bernie Smith was very kind about the whole matter and didn't turn me over to the police, I was deeply embarrassed because now he knew about my crime and the evil kind of person I really was. I seriously considered moving to another town to get a fresh start, but since I was only ten, the job market proved to be remarkably tight. So, I did my time.

I avoided the restaurant and the grocery store as best I could, but finally my grandfather talked me into having a chocolate malt with him. While I was sitting at the counter, a frozen French fry came flying out from the kitchen and hit me square in the forehead. Right then and there, I knew that I was restored to the community. You don't forget moments like that. It was a French fry of grace!

I learned a great deal growing up—mostly from experience, things that shape and form you. I learned that small things matter. I learned about right and wrong. I learned that I was accountable for my actions, and I learned that making things right usually costs something dear. But I also learned from people like Bernie Smith that grace and mercy abound, and that these are some the most precious gifts that one can give or receive.

And I learned that we are shaped not only by our victories but our failures—maybe even more so. It seems that God is particularly active in those times that we come up short or fall, yet we resolve to get back up or make things right. It is in those times that we are shaped. We begin to put down deep spiritual roots, roots that can sustain us during the dry seasons and nourish us as we resolve to live a simple, sincere, serene life—one that honors God and reflects the sprit of Christ in all we do.

Sometimes I imagine Adam and Eve looking over a green hedge back into the Garden of Eden. How ashamed and embarrassed they must feel—having been caught in a lie and getting kicked out of the Garden. They must have wondered if God would ever speak to them again. Of course, that's our story, too, isn't it? All of a sudden, two frozen French fries come flying over the hedge and hits each of them squarely in the forehead. It was a moment that they would not forget. How good it must have been to know—to really know—that they would not be alone in this world. God was still with them, and he still loved them dearly.

And I think that King David felt the same way, too, when he wrote: "Blessed is the one whose transgressions are forgiven, whose sins are covered. Blessed is the one whose sin the Lord does not count against them . . ." (Ps 32:1-2a). And after the whole Bathsheba affair, he should know.

And not only is our sin not counted against us, but God goes around making extravagant promises to us about our future and loving us dearly in the midst of our failures. I have a feeling that the first thing the father did when he saw his prodigal son's silhouette on the horizon was to go to the freezer and put a handful of French fries in his pocket before breaking into a full sprint. Perhaps the only thing in this world that is better than being hit by a French fry of grace is to have the opportunity every once in awhile to throw one yourself.

— PART IV —

Practicing Faithful Habits

Prayer, Work, Study, Physical Exercise, Eating, and Sleep

IN THE FINAL TWO chapters of this book, we go back to the basics. In chapter 14, we will examine how prayer, work, and study, three quite common human activities, are really interconnected in very interesting ways, spiritual ways. In fact, we will look at the connectedness of all things, and how such a view of our surroundings and opportunities changes the way we see what is sacred and what is secular. Perhaps it is neither necessary nor helpful to divide our world into pieces. We will also look at study and work as spiritual practices, and how such an approach can change, challenge, and deepen the meaning of these daily activities. And what if we would understand and see study and work as acts of worship and grace-filled opportunities to serve, grow, and appropriate God's grace to others, as a way to use our gifts? Wouldn't that give added meaning and value to our chores? As you will see, I believe it does.

In chapter 15, we look at the three basic building blocks for physical health—eating, sleeping, and physical exercise. Clearly, these are essential for our physical well-being, and much has been written about their importance. Of course, this is true. But as it turns out, they are important for our spiritual well-being as well, providing a rich soil for our spiritual garden as we strive to cultivate a simple, sincere, and serene life. As we well know, all the careful planting and tender care of a garden will go for naught if done so in poor and depleted soil. And interestingly, bad weeds seem to thrive in poor soil. There is a lesson here for all of us.

As we conclude this book and our time working and praying together, we will end as the prayer ends, with an honest admission that if we try to do spiritual formation on our own, that is, if we try to form ourselves, it will neither be successful nor sustainable. After all, this is not weight lifting or a hobby or something to try on a rainy day; it's spiritual formation. God must be a partner in our efforts, and the good news is that God desires to be involved in this and every aspect of our lives. We are not made to make such a spiritual journey alone; we are made for fellowship. Early on, God looked at Adam and thought that it is not good for anyone to be alone. Of course, God was right. He is the vine and we are the branches, and a branch doesn't bear fruit unless it is vitally connected to the vine. That's just a simple fact of gardening, and of life, too.

The irony is that spiritual formation is ultimately both a gift from God and an intentional practice that requires your best efforts. Indeed, it's a mystery. The good news is that God does not expect us to be perfect, but to be faithful. We conclude with the acknowledgement that the way to make such a journey (or any journey for that matter) is to ask for the gift of God's presence, a gift that is freely given.

— 14 —

Prayer, Work, Study

Pray as if everything depended on God. Work as though everything depended on you.

—*SAINT AUGUSTINE*

Introduction

NAVIGATING THE SACRED/SECULAR DIVIDE can be quite daunting. I graduated from college with a degree in psychology, but with no specific vocational direction. My older brother seemed to know early on that he wanted to teach and coach, a clear calling, but I, on the other hand, didn't have a clue. For me, finding God's call for my life was a scavenger hunt. I've spent my life looking for signs and clues. I still do.

After college, I knew that I loved God, wanted to serve him faithfully, and felt some type of interest or calling to ministry, vague though it was. I figured that the only way to do this was to go into full-time Christian ministry as a pastor of a local congregation, the only kind of ministry I knew much about at the time. So, I enrolled in a seminary to obtain a divinity degree—and I was miserable! Actually, I did quite well in the courses, but my spirit was so empty, at low tide. I felt that there must be something wrong with me, so I went to a faculty member I admired and trusted and explained my situation. "You're miserable?" he asked. "Yup," I replied, and started to cry uncontrollably. This caught him off guard and embarrassed me at the same time. "What do you really want to do?" he pressed. "Well, if I could do anything I wanted to do, I would work at a Christian college and coach basketball," I forced out between sobs. "Well, then why don't you do that to the glory of God?" was the response. "You can do that?" I asked quietly. He looked at me with compassion, shrugged his shoulders, and said, "Why not?"

Why not, indeed! Somewhere along the line, I picked up the notion that doing ministry was sacred work, while coaching basketball or painting houses or working in the financial aid office were in the secular realm. They were valuable and necessary forms of work, to be sure, but they weren't sacred. If you really wanted to serve God with all your heart and mind, it had to be in a church setting. Certainly, praying is a sacred activity, but work and study? Aren't they secular—and often not very fun? We study to get a good job and work to make a living, but that's in the secular world. The sacred stuff comes on Sunday—right?

I've now come full circle. I truly believe that the distinction between the sacred and the secular is an unnecessary and false dichotomy. In God's economy, it's all sacred work. In this chapter, we will look first at the connections between prayer, work, and study, and then suggest three ways to think about these very important activities: as acts of worship, as spiritual practices, and as grace-filled opportunities. As we do, I think you will begin to see how these activities can become healthy habits that shape you in deep ways and contribute to living a simple, sincere, and serene life. As in the other chapters in this book, we will also examine a passage or two from Scripture for illumination, offer some words of practical advice, and end with some questions for reflection and discussion. I trust that the shaping power and dignity found in the most routine of activities will become evident to you, and perhaps change how you approach these undertakings in the future. We know this: what you do and how you do them will shape you.

The Connectedness of All Things

One of the maladies of the modern world is the way we divide and live our lives in segments, missing the connectedness or hidden wholeness in things. We divide the sacred from the secular, the spiritual from the physical, the week from the weekend, the rich from the poor, the important from the unimportant, our work from our leisure, even our public worship from our private faith. In so many ways, we live out what I call the vending machine syndrome. Most of us would never think of stealing or taking money that belonged to someone else. If I dropped a five dollar bill in your living room or left it on a library table, you would pick it up and return it to me without much forethought at all. After all, if you kept it, wouldn't that be stealing? On the other hand, if you put a dollar into a vending machine to buy a soda, and along with the soda the machine returned five dollars, tests have demonstrated that most of us would say, "This is my lucky day!" and walk away with the money, considering it a gift from the machine. Why? In the first case, we make a personal connection between the person and the money; in the second case, we see no connection whatsoever—even though we realize that the money does not belong to us. We do not see the persons who make their livelihoods by placing the machines, stocking the machines, making the machines themselves, or canning the soda, or the supply and distribution chain necessary to produce the raw materials, transform it into soda, and deliver it to where the vending machine stands. No, we only see a solitary vending machine, disconnected from the rest of the world. So, we apply a different set of ethics as if the two cases had nothing in common. Some money appears, and we take it. Sadly, I have to confess that I've done it myself.

I see the same type of differentiation when we think about prayer, work, and study. Far too often, we see these three as separate activities. After all, isn't prayer a spiritual activity, while work and study are physical or mental things? Surely, they cannot be deeply connected, can they? For me, the answer is yes; they are actually connected in profound ways. First, you can pray before you go to work or begin to study. In fact, there are many websites that provide "before the work day" prayers, and I commend them to you. Certainly, there is nothing wrong with breathing a prayer before starting work. And I have seen more than one student pray before taking a test. Obviously, this is a good practice, too, but I've often wondered if a prayer for focus and discipline before and while studying for the test may have brought even better results.

In addition, we can pray about our work or study, asking God to provide guidance not only for the day or the exam, but also for the general direction of these activities and the trajectory of our careers, making them consistent with kingdom values. And we can even think of study or work as a form of prayer. What if we saw our desk or workstation as an altar, carrying deep spiritual significance? Perhaps such a stance would remind us that prayer, work, and study are interconnected in deep ways. I want to briefly point out three connections in this chapter: as an act of worship, as a spiritual discipline, and as a grace-filled opportunity.

Simply put, prayer, work, and study can be understood as acts of worship. To me, worship implies a sense of devotion and commitment, holding something with profound respect, reverence, dignity, and awe. Worship has a direction, too; it's not so much about me, but about praising God. It is easy to see how prayer fits into worship. In fact, pray is one of the common elements in most worship services, and has been so for centuries. But what about work and study, can they really be acts of worship—activities that glorify, honor, and give praise to God? Sure! Remember, these three are not isolated events, standing alone in the corner of the room like a vending machine. No, they are interconnected, all bringing glory to God. And surely, there is no need to confine worship to a certain place or assign it to a certain time of day (say Sunday morning at 11:00 AM). In junior high, I had a poster on my bedroom wall of a soccer player diving to redirect the ball towards the net. He was parallel to the pitch. It read: "All of life can be an act of worship if one desires to make it so." I liked seeing the player sell out in full layout position, and I liked being reminded that there is a spiritual dimension to our recreation and games, too. It brought a deeper meaning to the way I understood and played basketball in high school and college. It wasn't just about me or winning; rather it became an act of worship for me. As I look back, I think that I was on the right track. Surely, there can be a spiritual element to the things we love to do, things that bring us joy and renewal, but it took me awhile longer to recognize that all of life is connected—all of it. My work and my study are just as much a part of my worship as are my prayers, and equally important, too. This added understanding, it seems to me, carries an obligation for me to do my very best in all I do. I'm just not interested in acts of worship that cut corners or help me to just get by. In John's gospel (4:24), we are admonished to worship God in spirit and in truth. If it were up to me, I'd add "and in excellence, too."

Another connection between work, study, and prayer is that they are all, each of them, spiritual practices, disciplines that over time shape and form you in very beneficial ways. I believe that many of us have a very narrow view of spiritual disciplines—fasting, prayer, meditation, and giving to the poor. Of course, these are very good spiritual disciplines, but there are many spiritual practices available to us in our everyday lives. Take church attendance, for example. Young people are walking away from the church in droves, feeling that, in most respects, it is simply irrelevant or boring.

When pressed, many say that church just doesn't do anything for them. I get that. In fact, there have been times in my own life when I didn't see the relevance in church attendance either. A simple breakthrough came for me as I prayed "A Morning Resolve," which started me thinking seriously about spiritual formation and the practices that nurture and sustain it. It hit me one day that church attendance could be understood as a spiritual practice rather than the central activity that would meet all my spiritual needs and fill my tank for the week ahead. What a difference this approach made for me. Now, I attend, knowing that such intentional discipline will bear good fruit—in season. My work is to show up; God will do the heavy lifting.

So it is, I believe, with work and study. They are spiritual disciplines, too, and when you engage in them with the intention of being shaped and formed spiritually, and with the understanding that God is at work in and through you, you begin to tap into a deep spiritual mystery. Think of it this way: when you take the time to intentionally prepare the soil in your spiritual garden, pull the weeds, and carefully set the tender plants, they will flourish. You don't make them flourish; they just do. It is in their genetic makeup to do so. That's the way they are made. I believe that it is in our spiritual genetics to flourish, too, and not only when on a mission trip or leading worship, but also in our prayer life, our work life, and our study times.

There is one more connection between prayer, study, and work that I would like to highlight. They can all be viewed as a God-given opportunities to appropriate grace in its various forms. Let me explain. One of my mentors would tell me that the best place to find God's will was at the intersection of my gifts and my opportunities, and he would continue by saying that work and study are both gifts and opportunities. Thus, I should make the most of them. He loved to paraphrase 1 Peter 4:10 saying, "Use whatever gifts you have to serve others and you will be giving away some of God's grace." Wow! The first time I heard him say that, I had to ask for clarification. Do you mean that there are various forms of God's grace? Yes. And we can be part of the action? Yes. How? By using your gifts and opportunities to serve others, and when you do grace will abound. And since work and study are both gifts and opportunities, they are grace-filled activities.

Honestly, I'm still not sure how this all works, but there it is. This I do know: work and study are just as spiritual and just as powerful as prayer. They are all connected—as acts of worship, as spiritual disciplines, and as opportunities to serve and share God's grace in ways beyond our own understanding. They are all profoundly spiritual acts, shaping us as we strive to live a simple, sincere, and serene life. At the end of the day, there is no mundane or irrelevant life or task. We are, each of us, called to live as a faithful presence wherever we are and in whatever we do—to the glory of God.

Scripture

When it came to getting our household chores and homework done, my dad was fond of quoting 2 Thessalonians 3:10: "The one who is unwilling to work shall not eat." We tried on several occasions to point out that Paul wasn't thinking about us when the rule was made, and since it was written early in his ministry, he may have softened up a bit later on, but my dad didn't seem to appreciate the nuances of our argument and saw no reason to make an exception. We learned early on that work and study were not optional, especially if we wanted some dinner.

My father's hermeneutics aside, I would like to mention two New Testament passages that I have found to be helpful as I think about my approach to work or study. In both passages, I believe that you can substitute the word *study* for *work* without substantially changing the meaning of the passage. Remember, study and work are intimately connected.

The first passage is found in 1 Corinthians 3:12-13: "If anyone builds on this foundation using gold, silver, costly stones, wood, hay, or straw, their work will be shown for what it is, because the Day will bring it to light. It will be revealed with fire, and the fire will test the quality of each person's work." Notice three things about this passage. First, the list of material goes from gold to straw, from rare to commonplace, and from expensive to inexpensive, even cheap. From this I take that no matter the context of our work, whether making a speech to the UN or refreshing your flower beds with mulch, anything you do is worth your best effort. The habit of quality workmanship starts with attention to the smallest everyday details. Trying to save your very best work only for the big items is no more a prescription for success than trying to save your best performances by not practicing. Second, your work will be shown for what it is. The Day will bring it to light. In other words, your work (or study) will ultimately speak for itself—and it will say a good deal about you. Third, the fire will test the quality of each person's work. We will all face the fire from time to time. You can count on it. And when you do, it is quality work that stands the test of time. And since you don't know when or where the fire will come, it behooves us to do our best work all the time. There are no unimportant or throwaway chores.

The second passage, Colossians 3:23, offers sound advice as well: "Whatever you do, work at it with all your heart, as working for the Lord . . . ." I like this advice very much. Notice that *whatever* we do, we are instructed to do it with our whole being, as working for the Lord. In doing so, we observe and honor the spiritual connection of all things. I had the privilege of serving as provost at several very fine universities. At times, however, the schedule was overwhelming and the tasks bruising. During such times, it was both comforting and correcting to be reminded that this was ultimately God's work, not mine. I worked for him, not the university; it was spiritual work. Serving as provost was a spiritual discipline, an act of worship, and a grace-full opportunity. To be honest, it didn't make the daily demands of the job go away or the criticisms easier to take, but it did add a dimension of purpose and perspective that carried me through many a difficult day. In whatever circumstance you find yourself, work as for the Lord. It is a sustaining act of faith, and a mystery, too.

Some Practical Advice

Particularly in our culture, so many of us go to work each week to pay the bills, but live for the weekend. Somehow, there's a big disconnect between what we do during the week (some call it dog work) and what we do on the weekend (enjoy life to the fullest). I would like to give three bits of practical advice that aren't all the practical at all, at least not from this prominent point of view. Rather, they are practical in light of God's economy. As we have discussed several times in preceding chapters, in God's economy our values and priorities are often turned on their heads. Maybe this section should be labeled as impractical advice—or perhaps better, kingdom advice. Certainly, some reframing is in order.

My first bit of advice is to take seriously the reality that work, study, and prayer are not separate activities, but rather connected spiritual disciplines and grace-filled activities that shape and form you. If so, it is important to take work and study as seriously as we do prayer, entering into these activities with reverence, respect, and resolve, even if it is difficult to make the connections. If every aspect of our lives, including our workweek, study times, and weekends is holy, they demand our attention and our best efforts. God is present and at work, partnering with us in *all* we do. There need be no secular and sacred divide in our lives. Such a division robs much meaning and fulfillment from our daily tasks.

The second bit of reframing has to do with study (or learning). Some of us like to study (we think we're good at learning) and others don't (we think we're not so good at it). Rather than thinking about being good or bad at it (another needless division), let's think about study and learning as an opportunity—a gift from God. Actually, we are all learning machines, learning things all the time. The crucial question is not whether we will learn something in the next year, but rather what we will choose to learn, why, and what we will do with it. When we approach study as a way to worship God, a way to learn more about his creation, his church, and his character, a deep spiritual significance will emerge. If we enter into learning opportunities prayerfully and carefully, seeing them as an expression of our confidence in God's presence and guidance, they become acts of faith. Who can tell where such dedicated learning will lead? I can't tell you the specifics, but I do guarantee that it was take you somewhere, and shape you along the way.

The final bit of practical advice is to make it a regular habit to pray specifically for your work and study each day, and take some time to listen, too. Far too often, our prayers are petitions and instructions for God, rather than opportunities to hear from God. Take time to ask God to speak to you about what you are doing with your time, your talents, and your opportunities. Ask God to help you recognize opportunities that are before you, and ask for wise friends and mentors who can assist you as you work to reframe your approach to work, study, and prayer. Look for the hidden wholeness in all things, see the connections rather than the divisions in life, listen for God's voice, and follow his direction. When we listen to our lives, we are listening to God, too. After all, he is the creator, sustainer, and partner in all we do. And all we do has a spiritual connection.

Conclusion

In this chapter, we challenged the secular/sacred divide in our society and in our own thinking, seeing it as unnecessary and unhelpful. Rather, there is a connectedness of all things. We examined the connections between prayer (often viewed as a spiritual activity) and work and study (often viewed as secular activities), and highlighted three of the connections: as acts of worship, as spiritual disciplines, and grace-full opportunities. In short, they all have a deep spiritual dimension.

We then examined several passages from the New Testament showing the spiritual nature of common activities such as work and learning, and offered three ways to begin to reframe our thinking: begin to consider your work and study as holy activities; view chances to study and learn as sacred opportunities; and pray specifically for God's assistance in recognizing the spiritual dimensions of our daily activities, learning to listen to God's small voice. He is the creator, sustainer, and partner in all our activities, making them holy. As such, they require our very best efforts.

Questions for Discussion and Reflection

1. As you think about this chapter, what divisions between the sacred and the secular have you unconsciously made? What has been the result?

2. Can you think of an example of the vending machine syndrome at work in your school, church, or workplace? What is the result of such thinking?

3. How might your approach to work change if you thought of it as a prayer or an act of worship?

4. What learning opportunities are before you right now, and what has God been teaching you over the past three months? What would you most want to learn?

5. How has God's grace been extended to you through someone's act of servanthood in your community or church? What gifts do you have that you could use to serve others, too?

I will try this day to live a simple, sincere, and serene life, repelling promptly every thought of discontent, anxiety, discouragement, impurity, and self-seeking; cultivating cheerfulness, magnanimity, charity, and the habit of holy silence; exercising economy in expenditure, generosity in giving, carefulness in conversation, diligence in appointed service, fidelity to every trust, and a childlike faith in God.

In particular I will try to be faithful in those habits of prayer, work, study, . . .

— 15 —

Physical Exercise, Eating, and Sleep

There are people in the world so hungry, that God cannot appear to them except in the form of bread.

—*MAHATMA GANDHI*

Introduction

IN THIS FINAL CHAPTER, we will examine three essential activities for spiritual growth, fundamental disciplines for both our physical *and* spiritual health, yet they are so often overlooked or simply ignored: physical exercise, eating, and sleep. Why? Because for many of us, we see these activities as optional, unrelated to our spiritual formation, but as I will argue in this chapter, I have come to believe that in actuality these three are spiritual activities that have physical benefits, and not the other way around.

In "A Morning Resolve," we have been praying: "In particular I will try to be faithful in those habits of prayer, work, study, physical exercise, eating, and sleep which I believe the Holy Spirit has shown me to be right." From this portion of the prayer, we are called to be faithful to certain formative habits: prayer, work, and study (covered in chapter 14), and physical exercise, eating, and sleep (covered in this chapter) *that the Holy Spirit has shown me to be right.* How so? First, I believe that God speaks through Scripture, and there isn't a passage of Scripture to my knowledge that advocates going without prayer, work, study, physical exercise, eating, and sleep, although there are several passages that warn against overindulgence in eating (and drinking) and highlight times for fasting (but not starvation). And Scripture affirms the necessity of prayer and Sabbath, and the dignity of work and study. Second, Jesus modeled for us these same values, taking time to work, to rest, to pray, and to share a meal. He also made sure on several occasions that others had enough food to eat, and he taught us all to pray for our bread daily. Third, I believe that God speaks to us through the disciplined study and work of others, too, including medical science. Since all truth is God's truth, we need not fear the findings of science. Ultimately, all truth will lead us to God. As researchers and practitioners work to understand more about the human body, they confirm and affirm time and again the necessity of proper rest, diet, and exercise. We pay a dear price when we ignore them. Finally, I believe that God speaks directly to each of us. All we have to do is listen—carefully and prayerfully. As I listen, I am constantly being nudged toward temperance, care for my mind and body, and compassion for others in physical need. Truly, the Holy Spirit, in a host of ways, has shown us that proper physical exercise, eating, and sleep are good; good for the mind, good for the body, and good for the spirit.

Physical Exercise

Why is it that when I get stressed at work or home, the thing I need most is some type of consistent physical exercise, but it is the first thing that goes from my schedule? On far too many occasions, I know what I need to do regarding exercise, but I don't do it. Why? I have to confess that sometimes I'm just lazy. I would rather sit on the couch and watch TV. And especially when I am tired, physical exercise seems very much like hard, unnecessary work. Yet, when I do get off the couch and take a walk or work in the garden, I always feel better for it. Why I don't remember that the next time I'm tired and stressed, I really can't tell you. Certainly, stress and fatigue do not bring about the best in me. They usually accentuate my lean toward laziness, and perhaps bring on selective memory loss, too.

Yet, researchers tell us that walking briskly even twenty minutes a day can significantly reduce stress, blood pressure, weight, colds, and much more. It seems right to me that we should work toward a healthy body as much as we work to grow a health garden—a physical or spiritual garden. Why would anyone be satisfied with a sickly garden if there were ways to bring health and vigor to the task?

And physical exercise can have a social or relational aspect, and a spiritual dimension, too. I walk in my neighborhood almost every day, and while doing so, I stop and speak to neighbors that I would not otherwise even see. Others I know exercise regularly with a close friend or small group. These times can be richly rewarding, times to strengthen bonds of friendship, celebrate victories, and share struggles together. And I often pray as I walk, sometimes for my neighbors, sometimes for my family and friends, sometimes for myself, and sometimes I ask God to speak to me. Truly, these are holy times, attending to both body and spirit.

So, since many of us have trouble with the discipline of physical exercise, yet we know that it is good for our body, mind, and spirit, which exercise is the best? Is it better to walk, run, bike, swim, play racquetball, dance, or jump rope? Should we exercise alone or in a group? Is it best to join a gym or do this on your own? Should we try to exercise in the morning, during the day, or in the evening? These are all good questions. As one wise university-level physical fitness instructor and good friend puts it: What exercise is the best for you? The answer is simple: any one you'll do. And I have found that when I think of physical exercise as a spiritual discipline rather than as a nuisance or drudgery, I'm more likely to lean into the task. And once I complete my exercise routine, I am always thankful that I did.

Eating

Most of us have heard about (and some of us actually practice) fasting as a spiritual discipline, often as part of our annual Lenten activities. It is certainly an old and honored tradition. Jesus talked about fasting, too, so there is obviously much to commend this practice, but what about eating? Can eating be a spiritual practice, too? Do how and what we eat have spiritual implications for our daily lives, and for those around us? I have come to believe that the answer is yes.

In the first place, eating is part of the care for the body. We have all heard about the consequences of a poor diet or overindulgence or obesity, and the importance of a balanced diet for our general health and well-being. Eating is a personal act that has imminent consequences. And we are now learning that a poor diet and unhealthy eating habits have consequences for our grandchildren, too. Literally, the sins of the father and mother are handed down to future generations. Their health is impacted by our eating habits! If this is true, and we have every reason to believe that it is, then what and how we eat have profound spiritual implications for us. Just like the decisions we make, our eating has a moral trajectory. As it turns out, we do not just eat for ourselves; it is a communal act.

And eating is not an isolated activity in other ways as well. Food does not just magically show up in our supermarkets or in our refrigerators. Now, food production is a multi-billion dollar, worldwide industry. There is an enormous food production chain, sometimes operating close to home but often stretching literally around the world. Where, how, and at what personal, economic, and ecological expense our food is grown, processed, shipped, and sold have economic and moral implications for all of us. It is not the intent of this book to outline any particular causes or concerns. However, I do want to point out that eating is much more than just nourishment, and I urge all of us to look carefully at the food we eat: where it is grown, how it is harvested and processed and by whom, how it is brought to us, and those persons and communities who are marginalized and hurt in the midst of the food production chain. Honestly, there are many. As such, eating is not only a communal act; it is a moral act, too. If we are to live a simple, sincere, and serene life, we must be an informed, careful, and caring consumer of whatever we eat and drink.

Finally, eating involves not only care for the body and care for the economy, but also care for the earth. That is, how and where our food is produced has environmental impact as well. Certainly, food production methods that leave the land barren, depleted, or toxic are not acceptable, even if the land is far away and the result is cheaper food. It seems to me that all of us must insist on sustainable food production, and be willing to pay a bit extra for it.

In this section, I have tried to highlight some of the personal, communal, economic, and ecological implications of our eating habits and choices. This alone makes the case that eating is a spiritual act, and demonstrates in yet another way the connection of all things. We do live in a connected world; the choices we make in our daily lives impact others, and matter to God. It has to matter to us, too.

I also want to highlight another spiritual dimension to eating, the act of breaking bread together. I am convinced that any time we gather and eat together, it is a spiritual act. I will have much more to say about "bread" in the next section of this chapter, so suffice it here to say that sharing food is an act of hospitality, whether offered to a neighbor or a stranger. Jesus often gathered to share a meal with his followers, with sinners, and even those who wished him harm. I can't think of a better way to make new friends, to deepen relationships, and to share God's love than to offer a seat at your dinner table and share some bread. It is perhaps the most powerful relational activity I know.

Sleep

As provost, I would often address the incoming freshman class and give some practical advice. I would tell these eager students that there is a four step formula for obtaining good grades: (1) go to every class, (2) do every assignment, (3) take every test, and (4) sleep—preferably at night! You see, campus culture in the residence halls is not necessarily conducive to going to bed at a reasonable hour or getting up for early morning classes. Literally, for many college freshmen, the day starts at 11:00 AM and ends at about 4:00 or 5:00 AM the next. Sadly, many college students hit the wall about eight or nine weeks into their first semester, their bodies totally run down, suffering from fatigue, colds, flu, headaches, depression, and so much more. I am convinced that we are created for rest, preferably at night.

And if that isn't a clear enough example of the importance of adequate rest in our own lives, think on this. Doctors report that more heart attacks happen on Monday than on any other day of the week. And which Monday of the year has the most heart attacks? You guessed it—the Monday after we move our clocks ahead one hour for daylight savings time in the spring. And it is one of the most dangerous driving days of the year, too. All this fallout with only the loss of one hour of sleep. Rest is important!

Early on, the importance of rest was underscored in Scripture, and we were given very specific instructions. In the creation account in Genesis, God rested on the seventh day, and the Mosaic laws instructed God's children to do the same—to incorporate a pattern of work *and* rest into their lives. I have come to believe that the rhythm of rest is very important for us, too. We know that we can't plant a crop in July and hope to harvest in August. The growing process takes time. So does our recovery and renewal processes. We can't work for fifty weeks, and then hope to recover by vegetating for one or two weeks, or work the entire week and then veg on the weekend. Rather, we need to carefully and thoughtfully build Sabbath times into each day, each week, and each month. If we do, the cycle of rest, that for which we were created, will be natural, nourishing, and renewing.

More will be said about this practice in the practical advice section of this chapter.

Scripture

When Jesus taught on prayer, he instructed all of us to pray for bread, our daily bread. "Give us today our daily bread" (Matt 6:11). He taught his disciples to do the same in Luke 11:3. Was Jesus referring to spiritual or physical bread? Most biblical scholars agree that he meant both. Let's talk first about the kind of bread that we eat for dinner. First, since bread is such a common staple in so many diets around the world, it is easy to envision daily bread as the loaf of bread that you buy in the local grocery story or bake at home. Indeed, this is daily bread, but it is probably fair to say that the meaning of daily bread includes all the food groups you eat, not just the starches. Jesus simply instructs us to ask for the food we need to live. This, it seems to me, is one of the most basic and essential prayers anyone can pray. Please give us the bread we need for today.

And it is today's bread that we are instructed to ask for, not for the week ahead or this month, but for today. I don't think that this means that planning a menu of the week is wrong or having a pantry is a bad thing, but it is clear that the focus should be on this day. Give us *today* our *daily* bread. It is easy to forget the urgency of this prayer if we live in a land of plenty, but for most of the world, this is no trivial matter. It would do us all well if we were to think clearly and carefully about all that we have, and be grateful for that which sustains us today, our daily bread. In abundance, today can easily get lost.

The other word that is often overlooked in this request, "Give us today our daily bread," is the word *us*. Throughout the entire prayer, there is no mention of "me" or "I"; rather, the words are "us," "our," and "we." The Lord's Prayer is a communal prayer; we pray this together and for each other. Now the reason for the instruction to request our daily bread becomes even clearer. We are not only praying for our own daily bread, but for our neighbor's daily bread, too. I don't see how we can earnestly pray such a prayer each day and watch others go hungry. This prayer, it seems to me, compels us to action.

Of course, even as we are instructed to ask for our daily bread, we are reminded that we do not live by bread alone. When Jesus was hungry in the wilderness, the tempter reminded him that he had the power to turn stones into bread. Jesus responded by quoting Deuteronomy, "Man does not live by bread alone" (Deut 8:3; Matt 4:4). Please note, this response does not imply that we are not to eat bread or that daily bread is unnecessary or unimportant. Of course, it is! It simply says that we are not to live by bread *alone*. That is to say, we are to attend to the spiritual dimensions of our lives, too. Feeding the spirit is as important as feeding the body. This is what we have been striving to do as we have prayed and practiced the disciplines throughout this book. The mystery of it all is that feeding the body and the spirit are closely related activities, and sometimes they are the same thing. That is to say, when we offer bread to the hungry or break bread together around the dinner table or during the Eucharist, they are all spiritual acts of worship.

Ultimately, Jesus confessed that he is the bread of life (Matt 6:35), and he can nourish a hunger that is much deeper than the kind that comes for missing lunch. At the same time, as Gandhi observed, "There are people in the world so hungry, that God cannot appear to them except in the form of bread." It befits us once again to pray: Give us today our daily bread—bread in all its dimensions. Indeed, it is a wonderful mystery.

Some Practical Advice

Before we end this chapter, I would like to offer several words of practical advice regarding faithfully engendering habits of physical exercise, eating, and sleep—which God, through so many means and in so many ways, has shown us to be right (to paraphrase "A Morning Resolve"). In terms of physical exercise, the key words are doable, regular, simple, short, and fun. We have all seen joggers painfully making their way down the street or cyclists making their way up a steep incline. This is not the way to start a physical exercise program leading to a simple, sincere, and serene life. The first step is to do something that is consistently doable, and it is good to start with something that doesn't necessitate the purchase of $2500 worth of equipment and clothing to begin. Keep it simple and doable. Walking has been dubbed the golden exercise. It's a wonderful place to start. It can be done each day, almost anywhere, with almost anyone, and in thirty minutes or less. Just be sure to carve out time each day, make an appointment with yourself, and stick with it. Exercise time is just as important as the meeting with your boss. And be creative about how to make exercise fun. It doesn't have to be dog work. Often, having an exercise partner or group can make the time more meaningful and enjoyable, and it makes you less likely to skip a day since you know that others are counting on you and cheering for you, too.

Pay particular attention to the food you eat, where it comes from, how it is produced and harvested, and who does the heavy lifting along the way. My advice is to think globally, but eat locally when you can. And I am aware that there are a lot of agendas, politics, issues, causes, concerns, and personal and institutional campaigns surrounding the entire food production industry. If a cause does catch you interest, then by all means, get involved. There is not reason to withhold your voice. Part of living a sincere life means getting involved in causes that you deem important.

In addition to finding your voice, I would advise that you find a regular time and place to break bread together with those in need, and that would be in any community I can think of. Find a church or nonprofit organization that feeds the hungry and volunteer once a week or month. Be faithful to the commitment, and you will see and learn much about parts of your own community that usually go unseen, and you will be changed, too. Simply ask God to speak to you through those experiences, listen, and do what he says. It is a formative spiritual practice.

Get out your monthly calendar, look ahead, and mark out a day each month for Sabbath, a time for rest and renewal. It doesn't have to be a Sunday, but it could be. For some, this day is an unplanned day. You sleep in a bit, get a coffee, go see a movie with a friend, take a walk, enjoy the sunset, or whatever you do that fills your spirit. For others, this day has a to-do list of your own making. For example, I love to have a day to run around in my pickup with the windows down and some country music playing, crossing off items from my list: recycle, drop off the lawn mower for service, pick up some lawn fertilizer, and restock my stash of batteries and light bulbs. I often take the long way home and drive by a beaver pond and check out their latest work. In one sense, I am busy all day, but in a larger sense, I am rested and full of life. For my wife, it is a day at the ocean. She always finds a walk along the beach life-giving. And for others, it is unstructured family time. The key, it seems to me, is to intentionally mark out some time in advance, guard the time fiercely, and be intentional about doing things that bring you peace, rest, and renewal. At the end of a Sabbath day, your tank should be full, not empty.

Conclusion

In this chapter, we examined three spiritual practices that are often over-looked, ignored, or thought of as merely routine activities: physical exercise, eating, and sleep. Of course, these are activities that affect our physical health, but they have profound spiritual implications, too. That is why God, in a variety of ways, has shown us both the necessity for and the implications of these spiritual disciplines. A proper understanding and practice of these important disciplines will certainly help us to live a simple, sincere, and serene life. They are to be taken seriously.

We examined in Scripture the implications of Jesus' instructions for all of us to pray and ask for our daily bread, and noted that we do not live by loaves of bread alone (physical food). Ultimately, Jesus is the bread of life, implying much more than just that which is sold in the local bakery. We also examined our call to break bread together, and to share with those who have no bread.

Finally, I offered some practical words of advice: recognize the spiritual, social, economic, and ecological dimensions of food, and if prompted, find your voice and get involved at some level; be intentional about breaking bread together and sharing with those in need; find a physical exercise that you will do regularly, and do it; and make it a habit to find Sabbath times each day, week, and month, thinking of Sabbath as more than just the day when we go to church or sleep in.

At the end of the day, eating, sleep, and physical exercise are such common activities that their importance can be easily overlooked and go unappreciated. Yet when approached as spiritual disciplines, the profound implications for our own lives and the lives of those around us can be better understood, and it compels us to be mindful, intentional, faithful, and prayerful in our resolve to live a simple, sincere, and serene life. As it turns out, all of life is connected and even the most mundane daily activities have implications for the kingdom.

Questions for Discussion and Reflection

1. When it comes to physical exercise, eating, and sleep, which activity is most difficult for you to consistently practice? Why do you think this is so?

2. Do you agree that physical exercise, eating, and sleep are connected spiritual activities? Why or why not?

3. What does "breaking bread together" mean to you? What are three ways that you could start the practice of breaking bread with your neighbors (however you define neighbor)?

4. What would a perfect Sabbath day look like for you?

5. In this chapter, we have highlighted some ways that God speaks to us. How does God speak to you, into your life? What could you do to improve the acoustics?

I will try this day to live a simple, sincere, and serene life, repelling promptly every thought of discontent, anxiety, discouragement, impurity, and self-seeking; cultivating cheerfulness, magnanimity, charity, and the habit of holy silence; exercising economy in expenditure, generosity in giving, carefulness in conversation, diligence in appointed service, fidelity to every trust, and a childlike faith in God.

In particular I will try to be faithful in those habits of prayer, work, study, physical exercise, eating, and sleep which I believe the Holy Spirit has shown me to be right . . .

— CONCLUSION —

A Tended Garden Will Bear Fruit

Pray for a good harvest, but continue to hoe.

—*ANONYMOUS*

AND AS I CANNOT *in my own strength do this, nor even with a hope of success attempt it, I look to thee, O Lord God my Father, in Jesus my Savior, and ask for the gift of the Holy Spirit.* This, of course, is how "A Morning Resolve" ends, with the confession that we do not do this work in our own strength. Spiritual growth is always a divine partnership. In our own spiritual gardens, we pray for a flourishing good harvest, but we are obligated to do some hoeing, too.

As we conclude this book, we also confess that we depend on God's spirit, God's direction, God's fellowship, and God's strength as we strive to live a simple, sincere, and serene life. We do not have to do this on our own strength, and, in fact, as the prayer makes clear, we cannot. Throughout this book, I have used the image of working to establish and grow a vibrant spiritual garden as a metaphor for crafting a simple, sincere, and serene life. I earnestly believe that we can do this, but as the Gospel of John clearly reminds us, Jesus is the vine and the Father is the gardener (John 15:1). We are the branches (15:5), and no branch can bear fruit if it is disconnected from the life-giving vine. It is good to keep this reality in mind.

As you have read and worked through this book, I'm sure that some of my own personal convictions and theological commitments have been evident to you. But just in case you are wondering what I have been trying to say in the lines and between the lines of this book, let me be transparent.

For starters, I believe that we are shaped and formed every day by what we practice, by what we intentionally and resolutely do. Of course, we are shaped and formed every day whether we are intentional or not, but we can be intentional about our spiritual formation. And God is eager to partner with us, and, in fact, guide us as we strive to live a simple, sincere, and serene life.

I believe that God does not expect us to be perfect, which is good news since we are not; in some way or another, we are all broken pots. Rather, we are called to be faithful. That we can be. And even if we do fall, we can get up and move on. God is with us in our failures as well as our successes, bringing grace and healing and hope to all our endeavors.

I believe that the values and priorities in God's economy are vastly different from our present social and economic values. Whereas the dominant social values are appearance, achievement, and affluence, in God's economy, kingdom values of character, compassion, and community take center stage. A simple, sincere, and serene life is grounded on these values.

I believe we are called to live as a faithful presence in our own neighborhoods and communities. There is so much buildup among Christians about changing the world, calling all of us to be world changers. Universities even tout in their promotional materials and mission statements that they prepare their students to change the entire world. Of course, there is nothing wrong with changing the entire world (as far as I can tell, it has been done three or four times over the centuries), but I would certainly settle for all of us to work to change our own neighborhoods, in effect, to change *our* world. I am convinced that the now-and-not-yet kingdom has profound local implications for the way we go about our lives, particularly if our resolve is to live a simple, sincere, and serene life.

I believe in the sacredness of all of life. The distinction between the secular and the sacred is arbitrary, unnecessary, and unhelpful. All of our doings, relationships, commitments, and concerns are connected and have spiritual implications—they are all sacred. Worship isn't confined to Sunday mornings. What we do on weekdays and on Saturdays is just as spiritual and spiritually formative as what we do on Sundays, perhaps more so.

Finally, I believe that life is messy; either it is, has been, or will be. You can count on that. Being a follower of Jesus is no insurance policy against calamity. But I also believe that God is faithful, guiding and partnering in our best efforts and in our failures. You can count on that reality, too. And remember, he calls us to be faithful; not perfect, but faithful.

I conclude with this benediction from Ephesians 3:20–21: "Now to him who is able to do immeasurably more than all we ask or imagine, according to his power that is at work in us, to him be glory in the church and in Christ Jesus throughout all generations, for ever and ever! Amen."

A Morning Resolve

I will try this day to live a simple, sincere, and serene life, repelling promptly every thought of discontent, anxiety, discouragement, impurity, and self-seeking; cultivating cheerfulness, magnanimity, charity, and the habit of holy silence; exercising economy in expenditure, generosity in giving, carefulness in conversation, diligence in appointed service, fidelity to every trust, and a childlike faith in God.

In particular I will try to be faithful in those habits of prayer, work, study, physical exercise, eating, and sleep which I believe the Holy Spirit has shown me to be right.

And as I cannot in my own strength do this, nor even with a hope of success attempt it, I look to thee, O Lord God my Father, in Jesus my Savior, and ask for the gift of the Holy Spirit.